INTRODUCING
ISSUES WITH
OPPOSING
VIEWPOINTS®

U.S. Government

Other books in the Introducing Issues
with Opposing Viewpoints series:

AIDS
Civil Liberties
Cloning
The Death Penalty
Gangs
Gay Marriage
Genetic Engineering
Smoking
Terrorism

INTRODUCING ISSUES WITH OPPOSING VIEWPOINTS®

U.S. Government

Mike Wilson, *Book Editor*

Christine Nasso, *Publisher*
Elizabeth Des Chenes, *Managing Editor*

GREENHAVEN PRESS
A part of Gale, Cengage Learning

Detroit • New York • San Francisco • New Haven, Conn • Waterville, Maine • London

GALE
CENGAGE Learning

© 2008 Gale, Cengage Learning

For more information, contact
Greenhaven Press
27500 Drake Rd.
Farmington Hills, MI 48331-3535
Or you can visit our Internet site at gale.cengage.com

LIBRARY OF CONGRESS CATALOGING-IN-PUBLICATION DATA

U.S. government / Mike Wilson, book editor.
     p. cm. — (Introducing issues with opposing viewpoints)
   Includes bibliographical references and index.
   ISBN-13: 978-0-7377-3875-9 (hardcover)
   1. United States—Politics and government—Juvenile literature.   I. Wilson, Mike, 1954-
   JK40.U84 2007
   320.973—dc22

2007036335

ISBN-10: 0-7377-3875-8 (hardcover)

Printed in the United States of America
2 3 4 5 6 7 12 11 10 09 08

Contents

Chapter 3: How Should Government Function in the Future?

Indulging in a wide spectrum of ideas, beliefs, and perspectives is a critical cornerstone of democracy. After all, it is often debates over differences of opinion, such as whether to legalize abortion, how to treat prisoners, or when to enact the death penalty that shape our society and drive it forward. Such diversity of thought is frequently regarded as the hallmark of a healthy and civilized culture. As the Reverend Clifford Schutjer of the First Congregational Church in Mansfield, Ohio, declared in a 2001 sermon, "Surrounding oneself with only like-minded people, restricting what we listen to or read only to what we find agreeable is irresponsible. Refusing to entertain doubts once we make up our minds is a subtle but deadly form of arrogance." With this advice in mind, Introducing Issues with Opposing Viewpoints books aim to open readers' minds to the critically divergent views that comprise our world's most important debates.

Introducing Issues with Opposing Viewpoints simplifies for students the enormous and often overwhelming mass of material now available via print and electronic media. Collected in every volume is an array of opinions that capture the essence of a particular controversy or topic. Introducing Issues with Opposing Viewpoints books embody the spirit of nineteenth-century journalist Charles A. Dana's axiom: "Fight for your opinions, but do not believe that they contain the whole truth, or the only truth." Absorbing such contrasting opinions teaches students to analyze the strength of an argument and compare it to its opposition. From this process readers can inform and strengthen their own opinions, or be exposed to new information that will change their minds. Introducing Issues with Opposing Viewpoints is a mosaic of different voices. The authors are statesmen, pundits, academics, journalists, corporations, and ordinary people who have felt compelled to share their experiences and ideas in a public forum. Their words have been collected from newspapers, journals, books, speeches, interviews, and the Internet, the fastest growing body of opinionated material in the world.

Introducing Issues with Opposing Viewpoints shares many of the well-known features of its critically acclaimed parent series, Opposing Viewpoints. The articles are presented in a pro/con format, allowing readers to absorb divergent perspectives side by side. Active reading questions preface each viewpoint, requiring the student to approach the material thoughtfully and carefully. Useful charts, graphs, and cartoons supplement each article. A thorough introduction provides readers with crucial background on an issue. An annotated bibliography points the reader toward articles, books, and Web sites that contain additional information on the topic. An appendix of organizations to contact contains a wide variety of charities, nonprofit organizations, political groups, and private enterprises that each hold a position on the issue at hand. Finally, a comprehensive index allows readers to locate content quickly and efficiently.

Introducing Issues with Opposing Viewpoints is also significantly different from Opposing Viewpoints. As the series title implies, its presentation will help introduce students to the concept of opposing viewpoints, and learn to use this material to aid in critical writing and debate. The series' four-color, accessible format makes the books attractive and inviting to readers of all levels. In addition, each viewpoint has been carefully edited to maximize a reader's understanding of the content. Short but thorough viewpoints capture the essence of an argument. A substantial, thought-provoking essay question placed at the end of each viewpoint asks the student to further investigate the issues raised in the viewpoint, compare and contrast two authors' arguments, or consider how one might go about forming an opinion on the topic at hand. Each viewpoint contains sidebars that include at-a-glance information and handy statistics. A Facts About section located in the back of the book further supplies students with relevant facts and figures.

Following in the tradition of the Opposing Viewpoints series, Greenhaven Press continues to provide readers with invaluable exposure to the controversial issues that shape our world. As John Stuart Mill once wrote: "The only way in which a human being can make some approach to knowing the whole of a subject is by hearing what can be said about it by persons of every variety of opinion and studying all modes in which it can be looked at by every character of mind. No wise man ever acquired his wisdom in any mode but this." It is to this principle that Introducing Issues with Opposing Viewpoints books are dedicated.

"In a single republic, all the power surrendered by the people is submitted to the administration of a single government; and the usurpations are guarded against by a division of the government into distinct and separate departments. In the compound republic of America, the power surrendered by the people is first divided between two distinct governments, and then the portion allotted to each subdivided among distinct and separate departments. Hence a double security arises to the rights of the people."

—James Madison, *The Federalist*, no. 51

The founders of the United States mistrusted governmental power because they knew, from experience, it was easily abused. Thomas Paine, one of the founders, said that "government, even in its best state, is but a necessary evil; in its worst state, an intolerable one." How, then, could the founders create a government where power could not be abused?

Separation of Powers

Ancient Greek and Roman political theorists had identified three types of government: monarchy, aristocracy, and democracy; however, recognizing that any of the three could become corrupt and thereby pose a danger, the idea developed that dividing power among all three types would prevent any one of them from becoming too powerful.

During the period known as the Enlightenment, which began in the seventeenth century and continued through the eighteenth century, political thinkers like John Locke and the Baron de Montesquieu recognized that government had three types of power—the power to make law (legislative power), the power to enforce law (executive power), and the power to interpret law (judicial power).

If all of the powers were held by one person or group, freedoms, in the view of the founders, would be in grave danger. As James Madison, one of the founders, stated, "The accumulation of all powers, legislative, executive, and judiciary, in the same hands, whether of one, a few, or many, and whether hereditary, self-appointed, or elective, may justly be pronounced the very definition of tyranny."

Therefore, drawing upon the ideas of ancient Greek and Roman theorists and Enlightenment thinkers, the founders designed a government with three distinct and independent branches—executive, legislative, and judicial—each with its own type of power. By separating these powers, it was thought, the danger of tyranny would be reduced.

Another way to limit concentration of power is by dispersing it among more than one sovereign. The U.S. government is a federal system, consisting of a national government and fifty state governments. By giving the federal government power over some matters and state government power over others, the Constitution creates a check on any one sovereign gaining too much power.

In the words of former vice president Al Gore, "It is crucial to recognize that our ingrained American distrust of concentrated power has very little to do with the character or persona of the individual who wields that power; it is the power itself that must be constrained, checked, dispersed, and carefully balanced to ensure the survival of freedom."

Alexander Hamilton, one of the country's founders, said that "the history of ancient and modern republics had taught them that many of the evils which those republics suffered arose from the want of a certain balance, and that mutual control indispensable to a wise administration."

Separation of powers is not meaningful if the powers are not balanced. Many of the essays in *Introducing Issues with Opposing Viewpoints: U.S. Government* argue that the balance of power among branches, or among federal, state, and local governments, is askew.

When Power Becomes Partisan

The judicial branch serves as a check on the unconstitutional exercise of power by the other branches. Montesquieu said that "there is no liberty if the power of judging be not separated from the legislative and executive powers." James Madison, one of the U.S. founders, said that the judiciary would serve as an "impenetrable bulwark against every assumption of power in the legislature or executive" branch of government. But Alexander Hamilton thought that the judicial branch was both the weakest branch and the branch most vulnerable to attack by the other two branches. For checks and balances to work, the judicial branch must remain independent.

But judges are human. Thomas Jefferson, another founder, said, "Judges are as honest as other men, and not more so. They have with others the same passions for the party, for power and the privilege of the corps. Their power is the more dangerous, as they are in office for life and not responsible, as the other functionaries are, to the elective control." Independence of the judiciary cannot, by itself, guarantee that judges will judge in a nonpartisan way.

Founder John Adams said that "the executive shall never exercise the legislative and judicial powers, or either of them, to the end that it may be a government of laws and not of men." But neither Congress nor the judiciary can enforce law. What happens if the executive refuses to enforce laws passed by the legislative branch? What if the executive disregards judgments by the judicial branch? Former president Richard Nixon once said that "when the president does it that means that it is not illegal." If so, is that really a government of laws and not men?

John Adams also said that "all speculative politicians will agree that the happiness of society is the end of government, as all divines [theologians] and moral philosophers will agree that the happiness of the individual is the end of man. From this principle it will follow that the form of government which communicates ease, comfort, security, or, in one word, happiness, to the greatest numbers of persons, and in the greatest degree, is the best."

Yet many Americans doubt that legislators are out to serve the public good. An October 2006 CNN poll found that 74 percent of Americans believe that Congress is out of touch with the average American, 58 percent thought Congress is focused on special interests, and 50 percent believe most members of Congress are corrupt. Seventy-nine percent believed that "big business" has too much influence in the George W. Bush administration.

What about the power of the people over U.S. government? James Madison, one of the founders, said that "wherever the real power in a Government lies, there is the danger of oppression. In our Governments the real power lies in the majority of the community, and the invasion of private rights is chiefly to be apprehended, not from acts of Government contrary to the sense of its constituents, but from acts in which the Government is the mere instrument of the major number of the Constituents."

Winston Churchill, prime minister of Great Britain during World War II, once said that the best argument against democracy is a five-minute conversation with the average voter. If the majority of citizens, due to passion or prejudice, want government to adopt laws that harm the minority or take away rights, should legislators adopt such laws? Is that pandering—or simply being accountable to voters eager to see their views and values adopted and implemented by the three branches?

As you read this collection of viewpoints about U.S. government, remember that you play a role in that government, too. As Thomas Jefferson said, "Whenever the people are well-informed, they can be trusted with their own government; . . . whenever things get so far wrong as to attract their notice, they may be relied on to set them right."

Chapter 1

What Is the Current State of Government?

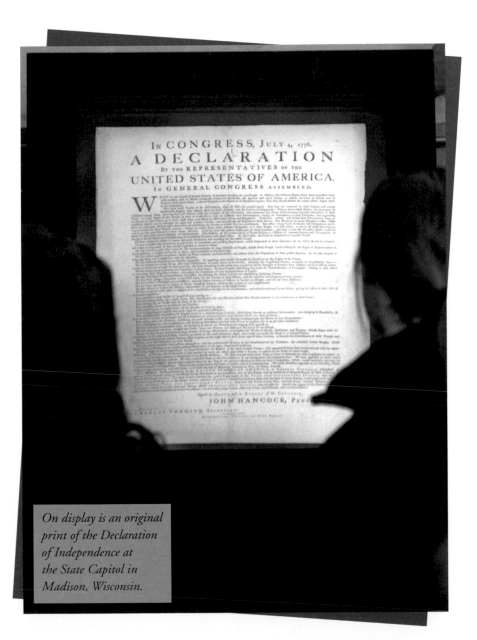

On display is an original print of the Declaration of Independence at the State Capitol in Madison, Wisconsin.

Americans Are Cynical About Government

Robert B. Reich

"*The public has turned even more deeply cynical about government than it was at the start of the Bush Administration.*"

In the following viewpoint, Robert B. Reich argues that Republicans mistrusted government before President George W. Bush took office but that events during the Bush administration have made both Republicans and Democrats even more cynical. Citing unfavorable ratings of both parties, he says both parties have been harmed by citizen cynicism. Reich is a former secretary of Labor and currently a professor at the Goldman School of Public Policy at the University of California–Berkeley.

AS YOU READ, CONSIDER THE FOLLOWING QUESTIONS:

1. According to the author, which party tends to be more idealistic about government?
2. According to polls cited by Reich, what percentage of voters think most members of Congress should not be returned to office?

3. What does the author say is the single most important attribute of conservative Republicans?

In contrast to a president's coattails that sweep his party to congressional victories, skunktails have the reverse effect. Bush's skunktails consist of abuses of power, corruption, and incompetence now so widely recognized that, according to recent polls, those who "strongly disapprove" of his administration now equal those who merely "approve." Because turnout in midterm elections depends largely on intensity of preference, Bush's malodorous tails would seem to bode well for Democrats who need to win six more seats in the Senate and 15 in the House in order to take back Congress.

Republicans Mistrust Government
But there is an asymmetry of consequence between Republican and Democratic skunktails. Even before George W. came to Washington,

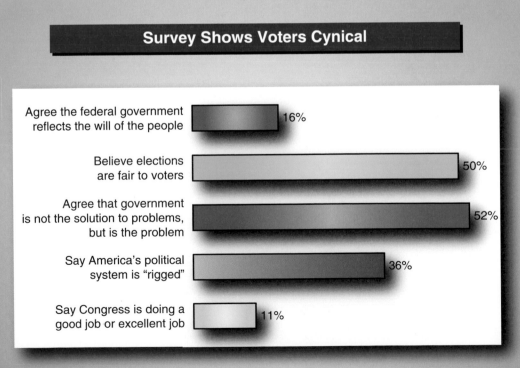

Survey Shows Voters Cynical

Agree the federal government reflects the will of the people — 16%

Believe elections are fair to voters — 50%

Agree that government is not the solution to problems, but is the problem — 52%

Say America's political system is "rigged" — 36%

Say Congress is doing a good job or excellent job — 11%

Taken from: December 2006 poll by Rasmussen Reports

Republican voters had low expectations of government. Presumably then, the fiascos of Katrina, Iraq, the Social Security drug benefit, the Bush fiscal policy, vote-buying and sweetheart deals with corporations, spying on Americans, Abu Ghraib, and the Dubai port deal, to list only a few of the misadventures [since Bush took office], have not especially shocked Republicans. They have confirmed established Republican dogma that government cannot do anything well and is not to be trusted. Democratic voters' aspirations for government are higher. Although Democrats have not shared Bush's goals, the overall ineptitude and self-dealing that has marked his efforts may have caused Democratic voters to become more disillusioned about the capacities of government in general, thereby jeopardizing Democratic aspirants for Congress as much as Republican incumbents.

Bipartisan Cynicism

Recent polls from the Pew Research Center seem to confirm this. The public's negative feelings toward Congress are high and strikingly nonpartisan. Unfavorable ratings of both parties are at their highest levels since 1992, and the view of Congress as an institution is at its lowest point in over a decade—47 percent viewing it unfavorably and only 44 percent favorable. This marks a major change from as recently as January 2001, when 64 percent of the public expressed a favorable view of Congress.

Anti-Incumbent

Anti-incumbent sentiments are running unusually high regardless of party affiliation. Forty-nine percent of registered voters say most members should not be returned to office, up from 38 percent in October 2002. Thirty-six percent of independents say they don't want the incumbent in their district reelected. That's as high a level as it was in October of 1994, just before Congress flipped to Republican control. But disgruntlement also runs high in Democratic ranks

President George W. Bush and his cabinet are subject to scrutiny and cynicism by the public they represent.

even within traditionally Democratic districts. Fully 31 percent of Democrats believe their representative should not be reelected, compared to nearly 20 percent in previous midterms. Only 18 percent of Republican voters say their representative should not be reelected.

More generally, the public has turned even more deeply cynical about government than it was at the start of the Bush administration. Excepting the months immediately following 9-11, confidence in Washington to do what's right "just about always" or "most of the time" has plunged since Bush took over the White House. Only 34 percent of the electorate now takes this positive view, while 65 percent now say they "never" or "only sometimes" trust government to do what's right. (By way of contrast, in 1964, 76 percent of the public trusted government just about always or most of the time, while 22 percent never or only sometimes did.)

Cynicism Hurts Both Parties

Cynicism about government is the single most important attribute of conservative Republicanism. Hopefulness about government's capacity to improve the lives of Americans has been the defining theme of Democrats since Franklin D. Roosevelt. That the Bush administration has succeeded so dramatically in deepening the pool of cynicism will stand as its greatest contribution to the Republican cause, and its most lethal assault on Democrats.

Ronald Reagan told America that government was the problem, but, ironically, his presidency enhanced the stature of his office and of government. Reagan thereby reversed the cynical trend that began with Vietnam and Watergate. By 1988, the public was notably less cynical about government (58 percent trusting it only sometimes or never) than it had been in 1980 (73 percent), marking a significant setback for conservative Republicanism.

Public Trust Undermined

George W. Bush has not made the same mistake. He has demeaned his office, reduced the capacity of government to govern, and undermined public trust. His skunktails may reach some Republican incumbents [in the 2006 elections], but the danger is their stench may be strong enough to extend much farther, and for many years to come.

EVALUATING THE AUTHOR'S ARGUMENTS:

The viewpoint you just read states that disillusionment with government is bad for persons in both parties who want to be elected to Congress. Do you agree? Why or why not?

U.S. Leaders Can Revive Trust in Government

Nick Gillespie

"Knowledge of how the federal government is spending our money is a crucial step forward in. . . improving the func- tioning of American democracy."

Nick Gillespie argues in this viewpoint that three of the 2008 Presidential candidates are taking steps to restore Americans' trust in the U.S. government. He states that while they don't agree on many other issues, Barack Obama, Sam Brownback, and Ron Paul do agree that the public has a right to know how the federal government conducts business. These presidential hopefuls have all signed the Oath of Presidential Transparency, a pledge that will allow the public to view how the government is spending money, in hopes that Americans will begin to trust their government again. Nick Gillespie is editor-in-chief of *Reason*.

AS YOU READ, CONSIDER THE
FOLLOWING QUESTIONS:
1. Signers of the Oath of Presidential Transparency agree to two actions; what are they?

Nick Gillespie, "Calling All Presidential Candidates: Who Will Stand up and Be Transparent?" *Reason Online*, August 24, 2007. Reproduced by permission.

2. What is the estimated cost of the free, searchable database Gillespie describes?
3. What does Barack Obama say that this "historic law" will do?

Presidential aspirants Sen. Barack Obama (D-Ill.), Sen. Sam Brownback (R-Kan.), and Rep. Ron Paul (R-Texas) don't agree on very much.

When it comes to immigration, stem-cell research, abortion, health care, trade—you name it, basically—these three get along about as well as Reggie Jackson, Billy Martin, and George Steinbrenner did during the Yankees' legendarily fractious 1977 season.

Three Presidential Candidates Agree On Oath

But they alone among would-be White House occupants have signed a trans-partisan initiative that has the potential to radically transform not just the presidency but the way the federal government does business. Obama, Brownback, and Paul have all signed The Oath of Presidential Transparency, a pledge to follow through on two actions.

Moments like this one, where the nation comes together as citizens and government alike, make Americans believe we are all united.

First, signatories agree to conduct "The most transparent Administration in American history—a lofty, laudable, far-reaching goal. This oath signals that whether it's earmarks, directives, or ongoing management of taxpayer expenditures, the goal of transparency will be evident throughout all policy making aspects of your Administration."

Second, signatories commit their presidential administrations "to full and robust implementation of the Federal Funding Accountability and Transparency Act (FFAT Act) of 2006." The heart of that legislation, co-sponsored by Obama and Sen. Tom Coburn (R-Okla.) in the Senate and signed into law last year by President Bush, is the creation of a free, searchable website that will list every recipient of every federal award.

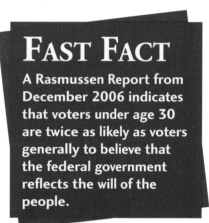

FAST FACT

A Rasmussen Report from December 2006 indicates that voters under age 30 are twice as likely as voters generally to believe that the federal government reflects the will of the people.

Citizens Will Have "Unprecedented Amounts of Information"

Regardless of ideology or partisan affiliation, this is something that every American—with the possible exception of lawmakers who prefer to shroud their activities out of guilt, shame, fear, or some combination of the same—can get behind. Estimated to cost a relatively measly $15 million between now and 2011, the searchable database will give watchdog groups, government reformers, and regular citizens unprecedented amounts of information about where taxpayer dollars are going and how their elected representatives are behaving.

"Knowledge is power," said Francis Bacon. And knowledge of how the federal government is spending our money is a crucial step forward in empowering voters and improving the functioning of American democracy.

The FFAT-authorized database, which will be operated by the Office of Management and Budget, is supposed to be up and running by January 1, 2008. But it's one thing to pass well-intentioned legislation and another thing entirely to implement and enforce it.

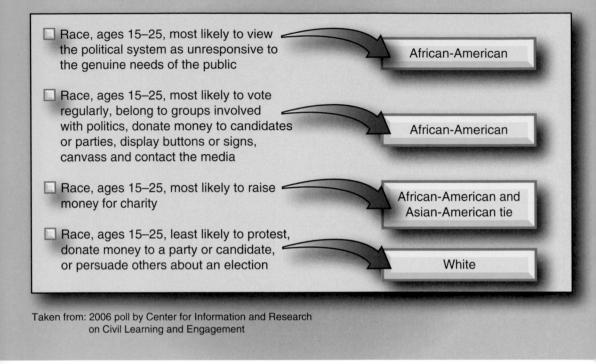

Political Engagement of Youth by Race

- Race, ages 15–25, most likely to view the political system as unresponsive to the genuine needs of the public → African-American

- Race, ages 15–25, most likely to vote regularly, belong to groups involved with politics, donate money to candidates or parties, display buttons or signs, canvass and contact the media → African-American

- Race, ages 15–25, most likely to raise money for charity → African-American and Asian-American tie

- Race, ages 15–25, least likely to protest, donate money to a party or candidate, or persuade others about an election → White

Taken from: 2006 poll by Center for Information and Research on Civil Learning and Engagement

Oath to Provide An Understanding of Government Spending

Hence, The Oath of Presidential Transparency, a project spearheaded by the Reason Foundation, the nonprofit that publishes the print and online editions of *reason*. Joining together three dozen diverse groups ranging from the American Association of Physicians and Surgeons to the Electronic Frontier Foundation to the voter-rights outfit Velvet Revolution, the Oath provides voters with a crystal-clear understanding of the candidates' priorities when it comes to government spending.

"Signing the Oath of Presidential Transparency was a no brainer for me," says Rep. Paul, the first candidate to put his name on the pledge. "I will aggressively pursue full openness and accountability within my administration if elected president."

"Every American has the right to know how the government spends their tax dollars, but for too long that information has been largely hidden from public view," says Sen. Obama, whose role in creating

FFAT can't be overstated. "This historic law will lift the veil of secrecy in Washington and ensure that our government is transparent and accountable to the American people. And I will be proud to fully implement and enforce this law as president."

Americans Need to Trust Their Government

"Americans need to feel they can trust their government," says Sen. Brownback. "As president I will continue my record of supporting policies that increase government transparency and boost confidence in our democratic system."

The Reason Foundation's director of policy development, Amanda K. Hydro, tells me that she has repeatedly contacted the campaigns of every declared presidential candidate in the Republican and Democratic parties who met Federal Election Commission filing requirements.

So far, only Obama, Brownback, and Paul stand in the sunlight by supporting transparency in government spending. As the 2008 race for the White House shifts into high gear, perhaps Hillary Clinton, Rudolph Giuliani, John Edwards, Mitt Romney, and the other candidates will take the pledge for transparency. . . .

Or perhaps they will see fit to stay in the shadows.

Which, in its own way, will tell prospective voters all they need to know come November 2008.

EVALUATING THE AUTHOR'S ARGUMENTS:

After comparing this viewpoint with the preceding one, do you believe that a transparency oath would enable U.S. leaders to restore trust in the government? Or do you feel that the cynicism described by Robert B. Reich in the preceding viewpoint would continue regardless of whether such an oath was signed? Explain your answer.

Religious Expression Undermines Public Debate

Ray Suarez

> *"Ringing phrases about what God wants. . . and assertions about being a nation 'under God' demand nothing of us as a people."*

Ray Suarez has been a senior correspondent with *The NewsHour with Jim Lehrer* since 1999, where he is responsible for conducting news-making interviews, studio discussions and debates, and reporting from the field as well as serving as a backup anchor. He came to the *NewsHour* from NPR's *Talk of the Nation*, and prior to that spent seven years covering local, national, and international news for an NBC-owned station in Chicago.

AS YOU READ, CONSIDER THE FOLLOWING QUESTIONS:
1. What does the author say is the difference between "God talk" and other policy discussion?
2. What does the author say is the Biblical punishment for disobedient children?
3. A story about a speech given by President Bush in Louisiana, recounted in this viewpoint, says that Bush's statement that the Bible is a guidebook for policy was insensitive. To what does the author believe the statement was insensitive?

Many people believe that the ideals of religion often cloud the issues of a political debate.

The difference between "God talk" and other policy discussion is that religiously tinged speech almost entirely releases a politician from accountability. The assertions are not checkable. There is no "other side" that can be put forward without calling into question the politician's sincerity and religious faith. A promise to reduce the budget deficit in three years can be analyzed and checked. A declaration that God has given the gift of freedom to humanity cannot.

"Checkability" is not some pedantic objection. When an elected official uses "God talk" as "policy talk," the intermingling of the two creates a kind of unassailability that is harmful to America, for people of all religions. When George W. Bush was in Canada for a meeting of the G-8, he got word that in the latest Pledge of Allegiance case the court had found for the petitioner, California atheist Michael

Congressional Vote by Religious Affiliation, 2002–2006

Religious Affiliation	% of Voters 2006	2006		2004		2002		Change in Democratic Vote	
		Dem	Rep	Dem	Rep	Dem	Rep	'04–'06	'02–'06
White Evangelical Protestant	22	27	72	24	75	25*	74*	+3	+2*
White Mainline Protestant	22	47	51	44	54	44*	55*	+3	+2*
White Catholic	20	50	49	45	54	48	49	+5	+2
White Other Faiths	3	66	29	57	36	52	41	+9	+14
White Unaffiliated	8	72	25	61	35	58	36	+11	+14
Non-white voters	23	75	24	72	26	76	22	+3	-1
White Jewish	2	87	11	77	21	67	32	+10	+20

Sources: 2006, 2004 and 2002 Exit Polls
* Estimates derived from 2002 Pew Research Center Election Weekend Survey

Taken from: pewforum.org/events/120506/green-bowman-tables.pdf

Newdow. The president pronounced the decision "ridiculous." I.atcr in the summit, during a news conference with Russian president Vladimir Putin (in some countries atheists can be elected president), President Bush responded to a question about the nomination of Harriet Miers to the Supreme Court: "We need common-sense judges who understand that our rights were derived from God, and those are the kind of judges I intend to put on the bench."

What?

Common sense. I am with the president there. Definitely a plus.

However, understanding "that our rights were derived from God" may not be a credential that can be assessed under the advise-and-consent clause of the Constitution. For a president who has declared there should be no litmus tests, that is certainly a religious test for public office that violates the Constitution. Wonder how the vetting process establishes these qualifications? I shudder to think of White House examinations of legal writings, educational background, and professional temperment also including questions regarding the

Congressional Vote by Worship Attendance, 2002–2006

Worship Attendance	% of Voters 2006	2006		2004		2002		Change in Democratic Vote	
		Dem	Rep	Dem	Rep	Dem	Rep	'04–'06	'02–'06
Weekly or more	46	43	55	40	59	39	59	+3	+4
Less than weekly	54	60	36	56	42	52	45	+4	+8
Attendance gap*		17	-19	16	-17	13	-14	+1	+4

Sources: 2006, 2004 and 2002 Exit Polls
* Attendance gap calculated by subtracting the vote of top row from bottom row in each column

Taken from: pewforum.org/events/120506/green-bowman-tables.pdf

nominee's belief that the laws laid down in Jewish and Christian Scripture trump the manmade laws of the Constitution.

A frequently asserted idea in these conversations is that the law made by legislators, reviewed by courts, and enforced by courts around America is fully consistent with the values of Scripture. People who say that must have their fingers crossed that the other discussant will not check or will simply take the allegation with a grain of salt. The Hebrew Bible and its Christian successors are full of notions that are simply noxious to the ideas put forward in American law. Some of the examples are trivial, some surprising. A vast document like the Bible, full of notions about daily life twenty to thirty centuries ago, cannot help but strain from the pressure of examination under the light of contemporary life.

For example, as we debate the wisdom of state-run boot camps instead of jail for incorrigible boys, and when to try teens as adults rather than children, we might consider this advice on juvenile justice from Scripture: "If a man have a stubborn and rebellious son, which will not obey the voice of his father, or the voice of his mother, and that, when they have chastened him, will not hearken unto them: Then shall his father and his mother lay hold on him, and bring him out unto the elders of his city, and unto the gate of his place; And they shall shy unto the elders of his city, This our son is stubborn and

Congressional Vote by Worship Attendance, 2002–2006

Worship Attendance	% of Voters 2006	2006		2004		2002		Change in Democratic Vote	
		Dem	Rep	Dem	Rep	Dem	Rep	'04–'06	'02–'06
More than weekly	17	38	60	37	61	37	61	+1	+1
Weekly	29	46	53	42	57	41	57	+4	+5
Monthly	13	57	41	50	49	52	46	+7	+5
A few times a year	25	60	38	55	43	50	47	+5	+10
Never	16	67	30	60	36	55	41	+7	+12
Attendance gap*		29	-30	23	-25	18	-20	+6	+11

Sources: 2006, 2004 and 2002 Exit Polls
* Attendance gap calculated by subtracting the vote of top row from bottom row in each column

Taken from: pewforum.org/events/120506/green-bowman-tables.pdf

rebellious, he will not obey our voice; he is a glutton, and a drunkard. And all the men of his city shall stone him with stones, that he die: so shalt thou put evil away from among you; and all Israel shall hear, and fear."

It is interesting to contemplate where in this country a state representative or senator might propose the death penalty for disobedience. The disobedience of a son is, after all, a violation of the fifth commandment, one of the Ten Commandments, which, we have been told again and again in political debate, is the basis for Western and American law. How long would the debate last? Would the Death for Disobedience bill make it out of the committee because legislators would be too scared to vote against it? Or would it, like so many proposals of its kind, simply expose the chasm between what Americans really want from the Bible and what they say they want. The same Americans who throng school board meetings demanding religious instruction cannot, by a vast majority, even recite the Ten Commandments.

A lot of the "God talk" in American politics is feel-good filler, unaccountable. Ringing phrases about what God wants, about his abundant blessings on America and her people, and assertions about this being a nation "under God" demand nothing of us as a people. Citing the Bible gets bellowing approval from audiences, but takes those same cheering throngs nowhere uncomfortable, nowhere challenging, down to no difficult debates about how we as a people divide our bounty.

The Reverend Welton Gaddy told a story that points out the problem with the political embrace of religion: "In the state in which my church is located, in Louisiana, President Bush made a speech recently. He went to an African American church in Baton Rouge, Louisiana, on Martin Luther King's birthday. In the course of his

Influence of the Religious Right

Question: Do you think the Religious Right has too much, the right amount, or too little influence in the Bush administration?

Poll	Date	Too Much	Right Amount	Too Little
CBS/NYT	Mar 2001	22%	31%	19%
CBS/NYT	Nov 2002	22%	39%	20%
CBS/NYT	Jan 2003	21%	44%	21%
CBS/NYT	May 2003	21%	40%	22%
Gallup	Apr 2005	39%	39%	18%

Taken from: CBS/New York Times poll, Gallup poll

speech—which turned out to be a lot about the faith-based initiative—he turned to the pastor, who was sitting behind him, and took the Bible from his hand. He held up the Bible, and he said, 'This is the guidebook for the faith-based initiative. This is what we're trying to do, because we're trying to change people's lives.'"

Gaddy's voice rises. "The Bible, a guidebook for a public policy?. . . Now, President Bush is the chief executive officer of this nation, pledged to defend the Constitution. He was speaking as a religious leader, not worried about the constitutional implications of that rhetoric. No president in contemporary America has the luxury of being insensitive to religious pluralism. It will divide religions in a destructive manner, and it will project ultimately a reaction to religion that will prove negative. The nation will be hurt and religion will be hurt."

EVALUATING THE AUTHOR'S ARGUMENTS:

The author in the preceding viewpoint says that "God-talk" makes people feel good but is not "checkable." What does the author mean? Why does it matter?

Viewpoint

4

Religious Expression Is Essential to Public Debate

Newt Gingrich

"The Founding Fathers, from the very birth of the United States, publicly acknowledged God as central to defining America."

Newt Gingrich argues in this viewpoint that the Founders of our nation, and the great leaders who followed, acknowledge God publicly as the source of our rights and blessings. Gingrich maintains that America cannot be explained without addressing its religious character and heritage, making public religious expression an important part of public discourse. Gingrich is a former Speaker of the House and author of numerous books on politics.

AS YOU READ, CONSIDER THE FOLLOWING QUESTIONS:
1. Whom does the author quote in support of the idea that nations have a duty to acknowledge God?
2. According to Gingrich, how did the first Continental Congress begin each session?

Newt Gingrich, *Rediscovering God in America,* Nashville: Integrity House, 2006. Copyright © 2006 by Newt Gingrich. Reproduced by permission.

The Founding Fathers believed that God granted rights directly to every person. Moreover, these rights were "unalienable"—government simply had no power to take them away. Throughout the dramatic years of America's founding, religious expression was commonplace among the Founding Fathers and considered wholly compatible with the principles of the American Revolution. In 1774, the very first Continental Congress invited the Reverend Jacob Duché to begin each session with a prayer. When the war against Britain began, the Continental Congress provided for chaplains to serve with the military and be paid at the same rate as majors in the Army.

Franklin Calls for Prayer

During the Constitutional Convention of 1787, Benjamin Franklin (often considered one of the least religious of the Founding Fathers) proposed that the Convention begin each day with a prayer. As the oldest delegate, at age eighty-one, Franklin insisted that "the longer I live, the more convincing proofs I see of this truth—that God governs in the Affairs of Men."

Because of their belief that power had come from God to each individual, the Framers began the Constitution with the words "we the people." Note that the Founding Fathers did not write "we the states." Nor did they write "we the government." Nor did they write "we the lawyers and judges" or "we the media and academic classes."

These historic facts pose an enormous problem for the secular Left. How can they explain America without addressing its religious character and heritage? If they dislike and in many cases fear this heritage, then how can they communicate the core nature of the American people and their experience?

America's Character Is Religious

The answer is that the secular Left cannot accurately teach American history without addressing America's religious character and its religious heritage, so it simply ignores the topic. If you don't teach about

Religious Affiliation of Congress (2005–2006)

Religious Affiliation	Senate	House	Total	% of Congress	% of U.S. pop.
Catholic	24	130	154	28.8%	24.5%
Baptist	7	68	75	14.1%	16.3%
Methodist	11	50	61	11.4%	6.8%
Presbyterian	15	37	52	9.7%	2.7%
Episcopalian	10	32	42	7.9%	1.7%
Jewish	11	26	37	6.9%	1.3%
Lutheran	3	18	21	3.9%	4.6%
Latter-day Saints	5	11	16	3.0%	1.9%
United Church of Christ/Congregationalist	6	4	10	1.9%	0.7%
Stone-Campbell	1	6	7	1.3%	1.8%
Christian Scientist	0	5	5	0.9%	0.09%
Eastern Orthodox/Greek Orthodox	2	2	4	0.7%	0.31%
Assemblies of God	0	4	4	0.7%	0.53%
Unitarian	1	2	3	0.6%	0.30%
Christian Reformed	0	2	2	0.4%	0.04%
Seventh-day Adventist	0	2	2	0.4%	0.35%
African Methodist Episcopal (AME)	0	2	2	0.4%	0.58%
Evangelical Free or Evangelical (not further specified)	1	1	2	0.4%	0.50%
Quaker	0	1	1	0.2%	0.10%
Community of Christ (RLDS)	0	1	1	0.2%	0.05%
Foursquare Gospel	1	0	1	0.2%	0.10%
Nazarene	0	1	1	0.2%	0.26%
United Brethren in Christ	0	1	1	0.2%	0.01%
Scientologist	0	1	1	0.2%	0.019%
Community Church	0	1	1	0.2%	N.A.
McLean Bible Church	1	0	1	0.2%	0.005%
"Protestant" (not further specified)	1	20	21	3.9%	2.2%
"Christian" (not further specified)	0	5	5	0.9%	6.8%
Unspecified	0	4	4	0.7%	13.2%
TOTAL	100	435	535	100.0%	

Taken from: CBS News Polls, "Poll: America's Cultural Divide", November 22, 2004

the Founding Fathers, you do not have to teach about our Creator. If you don't teach about Abraham Lincoln, you don't have to deal with fourteen references to God and two Bible verses in his 732-word second inaugural address. That speech is actually carved into the wall of the Lincoln Memorial in a permanent affront to every radical secularist who visits this public building. You have to wonder how soon there will be a lawsuit to scrape the references to God and the Bible off the monument so as not to offend those who hate or despise religious expression.

This is no idle threat. Dr. Michael Newdow, the radical secularist who continues to fight in court to outlaw the words "under God," told the *New York Times* that he intended to "ferret out all insidious uses of religion in daily life." While the Supreme Court did not find the words "under God" in the Pledge of Allegiance unconstitutional in the case brought by Newdow in 2004, Newdow has since instigated a similar lawsuit that has been successful at the federal district court level and is now on appeal to the Ninth Circuit.

Founders Acknowledged God

Unlike Dr. Newdow, the Founding Fathers, from the very birth of the United States, publicly acknowledged God as central to defining America and to securing the blessings of liberty for the new nation.

Our first president, George Washington, at his first inauguration on April 30, 1789, "put his right hand on the Bible . . . [after taking the oath] adding 'So help me God.' He then bent forward and kissed the Bible before him." In his inaugural address, Washington remarked that:

It would be peculiarly improper to omit in this first official act my fervent supplications to that Almighty Being who rules over the universe, who presides in the councils of nations, and whose providential aids can supply every human defect, that His benediction may consecrate to the liberties and happiness of the people of the United States, a Government instituted by them-selves for these essential purposes, and may enable every instrument employed in its administration to execute with success the functions allotted to his charge. . . . No people can be bound to acknowledge and adore the Invisible Hand which conducts the affairs of men more than those of the United States. . . . You will join with me, I trust, in thinking that there are none under the influence of which the proceedings of a new and free government can more auspiciously commerce.

> # FAST FACT
> Rep. Keith Ellison (D. Minn), the first Muslim elected to Congress, took his oath of office on a Koran once owned by President Thomas Jefferson.

The personal ideals of religion bring a great amount of passion to any political debate.

Duty to Acknowledge God

Then in the Thanksgiving Proclamation of October 3, 1789, Washington declared, "It is the duty of all Nations to acknowledge the Providence of Almighty God, to obey His will, to be grateful for His benefits, and humbly to implore His protection and favor." Note that Washington was not only asserting that individuals have obligations before God, but that nations do as well. At this point, the United States government was not yet a year old.

That most astute observer of early America, Alexis de Tocqueville, observed in *Democracy in America* (1835), "I do not know whether all Americans have a sincere faith in their religion, for who can read the human heart? But I am certain that they hold it to be indispensable to the maintenance of republican institutions. This opinion is not peculiar to a class of citizens or to a party, but it belongs to the whole nation and to every rank of society."

All Religion Deserves Respect

The secular Left and the media-academic-legal elite would argue that even if de Tocqueville were right, he is irrelevant because he is writing about an earlier America. They argue that America has changed profoundly and is now a very different country. [Retired U.S. Supreme Court] Justice [Sandra Day] O'Connor herself wrote that the phrase "under God" was adopted in 1954 when "our national religious diversity was neither as robust nor as well recognized as it is now."

Yet this is a profound misinterpretation of modern America. As [social scientist] Michael Novak has noted, recognizing one nation "under God" is much more important in a country as religiously diverse as America because the phrase transcends any one faith or denomination and is inclusive. Harvard professor Samuel Huntington points out that "Americans tend to have a certain catholicity toward religion: All deserve respect."

Acknowledging God Is Relevant Today

More importantly, the wisdom of the Founding Fathers concerning religious liberty is just as relevant today as it was in 1787 because it reflects a fundamental insight about human nature and how men and women might best live out the political experiment in ordered liberty that they ordained in Philadelphia.

The Founders had a very straightforward belief that liberty was the purpose of a just government, but that the maintenance of this liberty among a free people would require virtue.

And if virtue was to survive, it would require "true religion", which was any religion that cultivates the virtues necessary to the protection of liberty.

Implicit within this vision of the Founding Fathers is a pluralistic sensibility. Any true religion would be therefore deserving of the respect of the government, which would include the freedom to express in public the moral principles of such a true religion.

EVALUATING THE AUTHOR'S ARGUMENTS:

Compare the arguments in the preceding viewpoint with the arguments in the viewpoint you just read. Could both authors be correct? Explain.

Government Bureaucracy Is Not Effective

Joe D. Jones

"Government is just too big to be helpful."

Joe D. Jones argues in the following viewpoint that government bureaucracy cannot work. Jones contends that government is bloated and wasteful and that because of its bureaucratic red tape, federal agencies such as the Federal Emergency Management Agency (FEMA) are unable to respond to emergencies like hurricane Katrina. Jones is the publisher of the *Mississippi Business Journal.*

AS YOU READ, CONSIDER THE FOLLOWING QUESTIONS:

1. To the government of what country does the author compare FEMA's bureaucracy?
2. What does Jones say business has known about government for decades?
3. What is the author referring to when he speaks about "starving the beast"?

Russians with no vodka! Can you imagine that? It's true.

Before we look at the whys, it's important to understand just how important vodka is to the Russian people. According to a recent *Wall Street Journal* story, the average Russian pours down 9.1 liters of liquor, mostly vodka, per year while the average American consumption of spirits is 4.9 liters.

Production of vodka is being severely curtailed because the Russian government passed a new tax [in 2005] to help protect Russians from counterfeit vodka and then failed to make the tax stamps available to distillers. Apparently, somebody forgot to have the stamps printed.

Counterfeit vodka is no small matter since about 40,000 Russians die each year from drinking poor quality home brew vodka. So, the government's heart was in the right place, but they failed on executing the plan.

On January 4, 2007, the 110th Congress is sworn in at the U.S. Capitol in Washington, DC.

Bloated Bureaucracy

Sound familiar? Are there any similarities between FEMA and the Russian government? Yes, in fact, there are.

Both are bloated bureaucracies whose ability to respond is seriously impaired. They stagger under their own weight. Mississippians have become experts on FEMA's lack of responsiveness in time of emergency. . . .

We've all seen the news stories and know the situation on the [Gulf] Coast. FEMA won't bring in the trailers until the utilities can be connected. Utilities can't be connected until the debris is removed. Debris removal is a slow and expensive process. So, while thousands of Mississippians are without housing, thousands of FEMA trailers sit on a lot in Arkansas waiting for delivery.

Bypass the Bureaucracy

One solution to speed things up would be for the governor to issue an executive order, or the Legislature could pass a bill absolving construction companies of liability if they volunteer to move the debris. Such an order is known as a "Good Samaritan law" and we need it right now.

If not the governor, then the Legislature should act immediately to provide relief so that volunteer work can move forward. In the absence of a Good Samaritan order, construction companies can be liable for damage while they volunteer their manpower and equipment to help fellow Mississippians in critical need. Why has this not been done months ago? That's what a lot of cold, wet folks down on the Coast want to know.

Lessons from Katrina

Katrina has taught us many valuable lessons, and we will continue to learn more lessons for years to come. One lesson that jumps out is the quality of [Mississippi's] governor's leadership compared to the officials in neighboring Louisiana. Another is the effectiveness of the military in mobilizing rescue efforts compared with the federal agency charged with responding quickly in times of need. The most heartwarming lesson is the huge outpouring of money and volunteers that has rushed to our aid and continue on the job today. Americans do, in fact, care, and care deeply, about their neighbors.

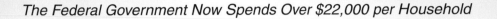

Growth in Federal Spending

The Federal Government Now Spends Over $22,000 per Household

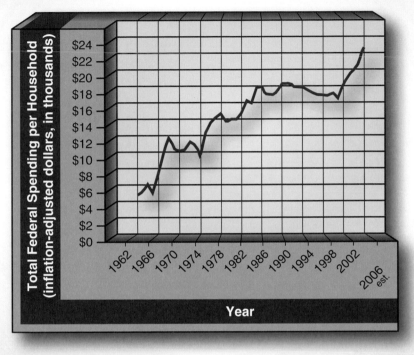

Taken from: Heritage Foundation

Why is the military—National Guard and regular armed forces—so much more adept at responding in time of crisis? Simply put, that's all they think about all day long. They drill and practice handling crisis situations and keep themselves ready to act on short notice. On the other hand, FEMA, now the stepchild of the Department of Homeland Security, practices how to look good in front of the camera and how to best disburse large chunks of money to both those in need and those who say they are, but really aren't. Money is an important resource, for sure; however, if there's no gasoline, food or ice available to buy, money is of little consolation. . . .

Big Government Doesn't Work

Katrina's victims and Russian vodka aficionados are learning the truth that business has known for decades—government is just too big to be helpful.

Useless bureaucratic red tape is always the hallmark of big government. Interagency turf battles, wasted money and unnecessary taxpayer expense is what we get for allowing our governments to bloat. For a first-hand experience you need go no further than the nearest airport and expose yourself to all the security smoke and mirrors that inconveniences citizens, provides unnecessary jobs for thousands of government employees and couldn't apprehend a sophisticated terrorist if their lives depended on it.

President Ronald Reagan had and [Mississippi] Gov. Haley Barbour [have] the right idea—keep taxes low and starve the beast before it consumes us all.

EVALUATING THE AUTHOR'S ARGUMENTS:

The author cites response to Hurricane Katrina as proof that government bureaucracy cannot be responsive. Does that mean that there are other situations where government has effectively provided services or performed tasks? Why or why not?

Government Bureaucracy Can Be Effective

Jacob S. Hacker

"The federal government isn't less efficient than the private sector. . . . It's almost certainly much more efficient."

In the following viewpoint, Jacob S. Hacker presents evidence that government delivers services more effectively and equitably than can the private sector. He contends that government services often become necessary because the private sector fails to make health care, retirement benefits, and other services available to many citizens. He also contends that the costs of administering such plans are much cheaper when done by the government than by the private sector. Hacker is a political scientist at Yale University and author of many books on government.

AS YOU READ, CONSIDER THE FOLLOWING QUESTIONS:

1. According to statistics cited by the author, how do the administrative costs of private health insurers compare with administrative expenses for Medicare?
2. Who pays more per service to doctors and hospitals, according to Hacker?

3. What government agency's quality control program does the author cite in support of his claim that the public sector is as good as the private sector in quality control?

In American policy debates, it's a fixed article of faith that the federal government is woefully bumbling and expensive in comparison with the well-oiled efficiency of the private sector. Former Congressman Dick Armey even elevated this skepticism into a pithy maxim: "The market is rational; government is dumb."

But when it comes to providing broad-based insurance—health care, retirement pensions, disability coverage—Armey's maxim has it pretty much backward. The federal government isn't less efficient than the private sector. In fact, in these critical areas, it's almost certainly much more efficient.

What Is Efficiency?

To grasp this surprising point, it helps to understand how economists think about efficiency. Although politicians throw the word around as if it were a blanket label for everything good and right, economists mean something more specific. Or rather, they usually mean one of two specific things: allocational (or Pareto) efficiency, a distribution that cannot be changed without making somebody worse off; or technical efficiency, the most productive use of available resources. (There's a third possibility, dynamic efficiency, but we'll take that up in a moment.)

Government Better at Allocation Efficiency

When the issue is health insurance or retirement security, allocational efficiency is really not what's under discussion. Nearly everyone agrees that the private market won't distribute vital social goods of this sort in a way that citizens need. Before we had Social Security, a large percentage of the elderly were destitute. Before we had Medicare, millions of the aged (usually the sickest and the poorest) lacked insurance. If we didn't subsidize medical care—through tax breaks, public insurance, and support for charity care—some people would literally die for lack of treatment. Market mechanisms alone simply can't solve this problem, because private income is inadequate to pay for social needs.

This is one of the chief reasons why government intervenes so dramatically in these areas by organizing social insurance to pay for basic retirement and disability, medical, and unemployment coverage, and by extensively subsidizing the cost of these benefits, especially for the most vulnerable.

What's usually at issue, instead, is technical efficiency: Are we getting the best bang for our necessarily limited bucks in these areas? The notion that the private market is, by definition, better at delivering such bang for the buck is the main rationale offered for increasing the already extensive role of the private sector in U.S. social policy. Thus, Medicare vouchers or partly privatized Social Security would supposedly engage the discipline of competition and lead to more efficient use of resources. . . .

Cheaper to Administer

[Government] programs are [also] ridiculously inexpensive to administer. The typical private health insurer spends about 10 percent of its outlays on administrative costs, including lavish salaries, extensive marketing budgets, and the expense of weeding out sick people. Medicare spends about 2 percent to 3 percent. And Social Security spends just 1 percent. Even low-cost mutual funds have operating costs greater than that. . . .

What's more, the government has another advantage when it comes to holding down costs: It is a powerful negotiator. Medicare pays doctors and hospitals less per service than does the private sector, and its costs have grown more slowly than private health plans over the last 30 years, despite huge technological advances in care for the aged. Medicaid is even more austere (some might say too austere): Its payments are well below private levels, and it negotiates bargain-basement prices on prescription drugs—something Medicare has been barred from doing. The main reason that Medicaid's costs are rising so rapidly is not that it pays exorbitantly for services but that it covers a lot more children and families than it used to, a good thing in an era in which private coverage has plummeted. Lest government's use of its

Who Works for the Federal Government?

General Schedule & Related (GSR) Representation, Fiscal Years 1996 & 2005	GSR Positions			
	Fiscal Year 1996		Fiscal Year 2005	
	Number	% of GSR	Number	% of GSR
Total GSR Work Force	1,393,462		1,425,499	
Men	714,161	51.25	728,508	51.10
Women	679,301	48.75	696,991	49.90
Hispanics	80,014	5.74	104,976	7.36
Whites	1,001,141	71.85	975,313	68.42
Blacks	234,488	18.83	247,285	17.35
Asian Americans/Pacific Islanders	53,325	3.83	69,823	4.90
American Indians/Alaskan Natives	24,494	1.76	28,102	1.97
Individuals with Targeted Disabilities	17,167	1.23	14,972	1.05

Taken from: Equal Opportunity Commission, "Annual Report on the Federal Workforce, 2005 Fiscal Year"

countervailing power to hold down prices seems illegitimate, it's worth remembering that this is exactly what HMOs [health maintenance organizations] and other big health plans were supposed to do—but Medicare and Medicaid do it better.

Dynamic Efficiency

To be sure, public insurance could still dampen what economists call dynamic efficiency, that is, innovation and improvements in quality. But in some areas, like sending out retirement checks, it's not clear where the innovation will come from, while in others, like micro-managing providers, it's not clear that the private sector's "innovations" are really worth emulating. Many of the innovations have to do with discriminating against people at risk of getting sick, micro-managing doctors, and shifting out-of-pocket costs onto patients.

Promises of government assistance lend proof to the idea that government bureaucracy is effective in serving the citizens it has sworn to protect.

Profit-motivated entrepreneurs quickly realize that the most effective way to minimize costs is to get rid of the people most likely to need care. This may be efficient from their perspective, but it's obviously not efficient for society.

Plus, when it comes to the most basic and important form of dynamic efficiency—namely, quality control and improvement—the public sector is arguably as capable as the private sector, and probably more so. As [writer] Phillip Longman has argued in an important Washington Monthly article on veterans' health care, the Department of Veterans Affairs (VA) has used its central power to create a model evidence-based quality-improvement program. Although the Medicare program still has a long way to go to match the VA, no one disputes that it conducts more rigorous reviews of technology and treatments than private health plans do. Indeed, private plans use Medicare's criteria for covering treatments as their standard of medical necessity. Information about quality is a classic public good—everyone benefits from it, but few have strong incentives to supply it. A large insurer with extensive data on its patients and considerable power to reshape market practice is arguably best positioned to provide such a good.

Government More Equitable

And this is simply to focus on efficiency. As noted already, the public sector runs circles around the private sector in terms of equity, the other major rationale for social insurance. If the current functions of social insurance were just turned over to the private market, vast numbers of people simply wouldn't be able to afford anything as good as Social Security and Medicare. Conservatives like to argue that everything provided in the Social Security package—the annuity, disability, and life-insurance coverage—could just be purchased in the private market. It could, but at far greater cost for most Americans, and many applicants would be deemed "uninsurable." All of which suggests that the claim that social programs are "inefficient" is often just a politically correct way of saying that they don't follow the usual market logic of giving the most to those with the greatest means.

EVALUATING THE AUTHOR'S ARGUMENTS:

The author's argument in this viewpoint is the opposite of the one in the previous article. After reading both articles, which author do you believe has the best argument? Why? What additional evidence would you like to see before forming your own opinion?

Viewpoint

7

Lobbyists Have Too Much Power

John Dickerson

John Dickerson argues in the following viewpoint that lobbyists influence legislators in ways more subtle than by campaign contributions. Lobbyists, he says, inform legislators about the issues and often give political advice. He says many legislators and staff also want good connections with lobbyists because they themselves will later become high-paid lobbyists. Dickerson is *Slate*'s chief political correspondent and author of *On Her Trail*.

"This system keeps everyone in cognac and cigars— and in office— if they follow the unwritten rules."

AS YOU READ, CONSIDER THE FOLLOWING QUESTIONS:

1. According to the author, how much did lobbyist Jack Abramoff pocket in kick-backs?
2. Why would a lobbyist not give a legislator bad political advice, according to Dickerson?
3. What is the real reason other lobbyists denounced Jack Abramoff, according to the author?

John Dickerson, "Lobbying and Laziness," *Slate,* January 5, 2006. Copyright © 2006 United Feature Syndicate, Inc. All rights reserved. Distributed by United Feature Syndicate, Inc.

[L]obbyist] Jack Abramoff's greed was so naked it's mesmerizing. He charged $750 an hour, pocketed more than $20 million in kickbacks from Native American tribes, and then called them "monkeys." Lawmakers who took the more than $4.4 million Abramoff gave since 1998, and their staffers, were greedy, too, though in a way that is more familiar: greedy for campaign contributions to get re-elected, greedy for fancy junkets, greedy for free meals.

But legislators rushing to make face-saving reforms need to understand that the problem on Capitol Hill isn't just avarice run amok. Lobbyists thrive in Washington not just because members of Congress are greedy but because they, and the staffers who work for them, are lazy.

How Does the System Work?

When I first started covering politics in Washington in the mid-1990s, my exacting bureau chief sent me on repeated missions to match campaign donations to legislative action. The information wasn't

As legislators listen to lobbyists, the American public wonders whether it is the legislators making the rules, or the lobbyists they listen to.

online then, so I spent days at the Federal Election Commission and the office of the House Clerk looking up who had given what to whom. I looked at votes and fixes in bills and tried to match them with the money lobbyists had given. It was harder than I thought it would be. Lawmakers rarely reverse field and support something they once opposed because a lobbyist said hop to or wrote them a check.

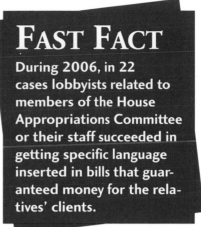

FAST FACT

During 2006, in 22 cases lobbyists related to members of the House Appropriations Committee or their staff succeeded in getting specific language inserted in bills that guaranteed money for the relatives' clients.

To explain the system, I turned to an actual lobbyist who had had a successful career on the Hill. Fortunately he was a family friend and took pity on a clueless reporter. We met where you would expect us to: a dark, smoky club filled with other lobbyists. One hour in that bar was more productive than all my endless days poring over tiny print in windowless rooms. The lobbyist's first point was that the dance of influence is subtler than people think. If it works right, a member never has to say, even to himself, "I have to vote for this subsidy because lobbyist Jack has just put a check in my pocket." That happens on occasion, but usually only when a piece of legislation comes up suddenly, or if a lobbyist goes off script. The more effective scenario, for everyone concerned, involves the lobbyist becoming friendly with members of the Congress member's staff, who research issues and advise him or her what to do and how to vote.

Providing Information

When the member of Congress goes to staff for information, he wants it fast. A staffer can read all available material on the issue, think through the policy, and balance what's right against the member's political interests—or he can call his friend Smitty the lobbyist. Smitty knows all about this complicated stuff in the telecommunications bill. He was talking about it just the other day at the Wizards [basketball] game, which was almost as fun as the Cointreau-and-capon party Smitty hosted at his spread in Great Falls [Virginia] over Labor Day.

Smitty has a solid, intellectually defensible answer to every question. He also knows how an issue is likely to play out politically for the member back in his home district. In a hectic day, Smitty makes a staffer's day easier. That's almost as appealing as the skybox and the free drinks [at sporting events]. It's easy to rationalize relying on lobbyists for this kind of help. In asking lobbyists to help them understand technical issues, staffers are doing the same thing journalists do every day—and in fact, journalists often call the same lobbyists for the same reason. They find someone who understands the issue, figuring that they're smart enough to use the information that rings true and discard the spin.

Giving Political Advice

At this point, I seem to remember my lobbyist friend gesturing with his cigar to emphasize his point. Smitty is not going to give his staffer

Poll Shows Who Americans Think Have Too Much Power in Washington

	Too Much (%)	Too Little (%)	About Right (%)	Not Sure/ Refused (%)
Big companies	90	5	3	2
Political action committees	85	10	1	3
Political lobbyists	74	17	2	7
The news media	68	23	5	4
Trade associations	61	22	3	14
TV and radio talk shows	51	34	8	6
Labor unions	43	46	4	7
Churches & religious groups	35	55	5	4
Opinion polls	33	53	5	9
Racial minorities	28	58	7	6
Nonprofit organizations	23	67	5	6
Public opinion	16	78	3	3
Small business	4	92	2	3

Note: Percentages may not add up exactly to 100 percent due to rounding.

Taken from: Harris Poll, Dec. 2005

friend bad political advice if he can help it, not because they are buddies and went golfing at Burning Tree [Country Club] together, but because he values his long-term relationship with the staffer and the member he works for. Smitty must provide an answer that helps his client but still protects the politician. Smitty wants to be called the next time and the time after that. In the back of his mind, he fantasizes about the member deciding he wants to introduce a free-standing piece of legislation that will help Smitty's client. That's not going to happen if Smitty hangs him out to dry.

This system keeps everyone in cognac and cigars—and in office—if they follow the unwritten rules. Abramoff didn't follow them. He got too greedy and pushed too hard. He didn't look out for the interests of the lawmakers he was buying. His requests were too explicit and obvious, and too closely linked in time to campaign contributions and excessive freebies. That's why so many other lobbyists are mad at him—they had a nice thing going before he screwed it up. When other lobbyists are quoted in the paper denouncing Abramoff, they're more likely to be angry at his lack of art than at his lack of ethics.

They Want to Become Lobbyists

[Capitol] Hill staffers have another motivation for relying on lobbyists, which is more long-term venal than short-term greedy. Many don't want to stick around and trade stories about budget resolutions at the House canteen for more than few years. They want to become lobbyists themselves and earn mid-six-figure salaries, instead of mid-five-figure ones. A couple of years on the Hill, and all the personal connections it brings, can translate into some nice offers on K Street [in Washington D.C. where many lobbyists have offices] down the road. Smitty isn't just your good pal today. He's your boss tomorrow.

EVALUATING THE AUTHOR'S ARGUMENTS:

The author describes reasons why legislators and their staff rely upon lobbyists. What rules or laws, if any, do you think could be adopted that might reduce reliance upon lobbyists?

Lobbyists Are Valuable and Necessary

Mark A. Hofmann

"Lobbyists are a necessary part of the political process."

Mark A. Hofmann argues in the following viewpoint that lobbyists perform a valuable service by representing citizens who do not have time to lobby Congress. The vast majority of lobbyists, he claims, are hardworking and honest. Problems of influence, maintains Hofmann, have to do with the way political campaigns are conducted. Hofmann is the senior editor of *Business Insurance* magazine.

AS YOU READ, CONSIDER THE FOLLOWING QUESTIONS:

1. How many dishonest lobbyists does the author say he's dealt with over twenty years?
2. Why does Hofmann think people have overreacted to the Abramoff scandal?
3. How do the election campaign cycles of other countries compare with the campaign cycle in the United States, according to the author?

Official Washington has entered one of its periodic paroxysms of self-examination, and it claims not to like what it sees.

What it sees is a city ridden with, gasp, lobbyists. Under normal circumstances, this fact of life wouldn't merit attention. But these are not normal circumstances, and lawmakers have responded in the time-honored manner of calling for something to be done, in this case something about lobbyists. Lobbyists are suddenly, at best, a necessary evil.

Hypocrites Criticize Lobbyists

Just as in 1980, when Abscam* rocked the Capitol, and in 1994, when the check bouncing scandal in the House of Representatives helped give the GOP [Republican Party] control of both houses of Congress for the first time in 40 years, the scandals of 2006—centering around one Jack Abramoff, lobbyist extraordinaire—have left many people in this city expressing shock and dismay. Their shock is about as convincing as Captain Renault's in [the film] "Casablanca" when told that gambling was going on at Rick's Cafe Americain.

For those who have somehow managed to avoid any form of news—including blogs—for the past few weeks, Mr. Abramoff recently pleaded guilty to a variety of charges, including conspiracy to bribe public officials. The particulars had to do with the actions of Mr. Abramoff, who claimed to be working on behalf of his clients, Native Americans with casino gambling interests. Apparently, he defrauded them along the way as he merrily pocketed millions of dollars.

Now, this would have been business as usual in a previous Gilded Age, although back in the 1870s Native Americans didn't have the wherewithal to hire people like Mr. Abramoff. Perhaps we have made some progress—at least now people who cheat Native Americans can be held accountable.

Mr. Abramoff's plea was part of a deal in which he agreed to name names, including the names of some members of Congress, as well as those of their staff members. People are nervous, and rightly so. And when people get really nervous, they tend to overreact.

*Abscam was a "sting" operation that caught several corrupt legislators taking bribes.

Ratio of Lobbyists to Legislators by State in 2005

State	Total Lobbyists	Total Legislators	Number of Lobbyists per Legislator
New York	4264	212	20
Florida	2148	160	13
Illinois	2264	177	13
Nevada	807	63	13
Ohio	1388	132	11
California	1162	120	10
Arizona	800	90	9
Michigan	1345	148	9
Texas	1703	181	9
New Mexico	860	112	8
Minnesota	1343	201	7
Nebraska	357	49	7
Oregon	607	90	7
Georgia	1404	236	6
Missouri	1130	197	6
South Dakota	645	105	6
Virginia	867	140	6
Washington	872	147	6
Wisconsin	753	132	6
Colorado	544	100	5
Indiana	700	150	5
Kentucky	632	138	5
New Jersey	613	120	5
Wyoming	479	90	5
Alabama	569	140	4

State	Total Lobbyists	Total Legislators	Number of Lobbyists per Legislator
Delaware	258	62	4
Hawaii	286	76	4
Iowa	651	150	4
Louisiana	509	144	4
North Carolina	620	170	4
North Dakota	625	141	4
Rhode Island	483	113	4
Tennessee	562	132	4
Arkansas	429	135	3
Connecticut	625	187	3
Idaho	300	105	3
Kansas	561	165	3
Maryland	654	188	3
Massachusetts	578	200	3
Montana	514	150	3
Oklahoma	415	149	3
Utah	309	104	3
West Virginia	405	134	3
Alaska	130	60	2
Mississippi	419	174	2
Pennsylvania	468	253	2
South Carolina	349	170	2
Vermont	357	180	2
Maine	199	186	1
New Hampshire	224	424	1

Taken from: Center for Public Integrity, 2006.

Lobbyists Not the Problem

The problem isn't the lobbyists. In more than 20 years of covering politics at both the state and national level, I can count the number of truly dishonest lobbyists I've dealt with on the fingers of one hand, with enough fingers left over to tally the number of really stupid ones I've encountered. The vast majority, both within and without the insurance industry, are honest, hard-working people.

Lobbyists perform a valuable service in a republic like ours. The average citizen has neither the time nor the money to spend camped on a member of Congress' doorstep in hopes of making a plea for this or that policy initiative. The citizens' interests, particularly their professional interests, need professional representation. That's where lobbyists come in.

That doesn't mean that the practice of lobbying couldn't use some reform. Government can always use more transparency. The public has a right to know who's paying whom how much for what. Ethics panels need to take their job seriously.

Perpetual Campaigning Is the Problem

But the real problem isn't lobbyists—it's what I call the "perpetual

Information from lobbyists may help legislators make better decisions for the public they have sworn to serve.

campaign." That's the endless election cycle that starts anew even before the loser delivers a concession speech. It's become an engrained part of Washington culture that invites the kind of dishonest antics in which Mr. Abramoff engaged. . . .

Other advanced democratic nations manage to choose their governments with remarkable dispatch, spending, at most, a few months on the campaign trail. If you want to see how it works, just look north—the Canadians are in the midst of what by U.S. standards would seem a remarkably short, if not particularly sweet, run-up to national elections.

Instead, we've got the political equivalent of a perpetual motion machine that demands a constant stream of campaign contributions for fuel, 365 days a year, whether it's an election year or not. The kind of money the overheating campaign machine demands can create both desperation and temptation for lawmakers, and opportunities for those who are less than scrupulous.

Bringing the perpetual campaign under control will require a cultural change, and it won't happen overnight, or possibly for quite a few election cycles. But doing so ultimately would be to everyone's benefit, including lawmakers, who'd have more time to focus on the people's business.

So let the lobbying reforms begin, while bearing in mind that lobbyists are a necessary part of the political process. The perpetual campaign, though, is not.

EVALUATING THE AUTHOR'S ARGUMENTS:

After reading this viewpoint and the preceding one, upon what points do you think the authors are in agreement and on what points do they disagree? Support your answer with evidence from the text.

Chapter 2

Are Governmental Powers Properly Balanced?

An official photo of U.S. Supreme Court Justices Thurgood Marshall, William Brennan Jr, Chief Justice William Rehnquist, Byron White, Harry Blackmun, Sandra Day O'Connor, Lewis Powell Jr, John Paul Stevens, and Antonin Scalia, circa 1986.

Courts Should Not Have the Power of Judicial Review

Jeremy Waldron

"[Supreme Court Justices] do not represent anybody."

In the following viewpoint, Jeremy Walden argues that judicial review (the power to declare laws and government actions unconstitutional) is undemocratic. It is unfair, he says, that a simple majority of justices can declare what is constitutional, but legislators, who represent the people, must have a supermajority to amend the Constitution. Justices who are appointed, he says, are not accountable to the public and are free to substitute their own values for those of the citizens, thereby undermining political equality. Waldron is director of the Center for Law and Philosophy at Columbia University in New York City.

AS YOU READ, CONSIDER THE FOLLOWING QUESTIONS:

1. Which Supreme Court justice does the author cite in support of his argument?
2. Why, according to Waldron, do people look to judicial review rather than electoral politics to effect change?

Jeremy Waldron, "The Core of the Case Against Judicial Review," *Yale Law Journal*, April 1, 2006. Copyright © 2006 The Yale Law Journal Company, Inc. Reprinted by permission of The Yale Law Journal Company and William S. Hein company.

In a system like the United States, we observe decisions being made not by a legislature but by . . . the U.S. Supreme Court on a vexed issue of rights on which the citizens disagree. And a citizen . . . who disagrees with the substance of one of the Court's decisions complains about it. She asks: (1) why should these nine men and women determine the matter?; and (2) even if they do, why should they make their decision using the procedure that they use rather than a procedure that gives more weight to Justices with a view that [the citizen] favors?

Law or Personal Philosophy?

These are much tougher questions for the Court to answer than they were for legislators to answer. We have it on good authority that challenges like these are often voiced noisily outside the Court and that the Justices are sometimes distressed by them. Some of them, however, reflect on that distress. . . . I am going to quote [Supreme Court] Justice Antonin Scalia and quote him at length.

> In truth, I am as distressed as the Court is . . . about the "political pressure" directed to the Court: the marches, the mail, the protests aimed at inducing us to change our opinions. How upsetting it is, that so many of our citizens (good people, not lawless ones, on both sides of this abortion issue, and on various sides of other issues as well) think that we Justices should properly take into account their views, as though we were engaged not in ascertaining an objective law but in determining some kind of social consensus. The Court would profit, I think, from giving less attention to the fact of this distressing phenomenon, and more attention to the cause of it. That cause permeates today's opinion: a new mode of constitutional adjudication that relies not upon text and traditional practice to determine the law, but upon what the Court calls "reasoned judgment," which turns out to be nothing but philosophical predilection and moral intuition.

Justice Scalia continued:

What makes all this relevant to the bothersome application of "political pressure" against the Court are the twin facts that the American people love democracy and the American people are not fools. As long as this Court thought (and the people thought) that we Justices were doing essentially lawyers' work up here—reading text and discerning our society's traditional understanding of that text—the public pretty much left us alone. Texts and traditions are facts to study, not convictions to demonstrate about. But if in reality our process of constitutional adjudication consists primarily of making value judgments . . . then a free and intelligent people's attitude towards us can be expected to be (ought to be) quite different. The people know that their value judgments are quite as good as those taught in any law school—maybe better. If, indeed, the "liberties" protected by the Constitution are, as the Court says, undefined and unbounded, then the people should demonstrate, to protest that we do not implement their values instead of ours.

So, as Scalia says, the legitimacy questions are front-and-center, and the defenders of judicial review have to figure out a response.

FAST FACT

A survey conducted by Syracuse University showed that 56 percent of people believed judges say their decisions are based on law and the Constitution, but in many cases are really based on the judges' own personal beliefs."

Justices Are Not Elected

First, why should these Justices and these Justices alone decide the matter? One answer might be that the Justices have been appointed and approved by decisionmakers and decisionmaking bodies (the President and the Senate) who have certain elective credentials. The President is elected and people often know what sort of persons he is likely to appoint to the Supreme Court, and the U.S. Senators who have to approve the appointments are

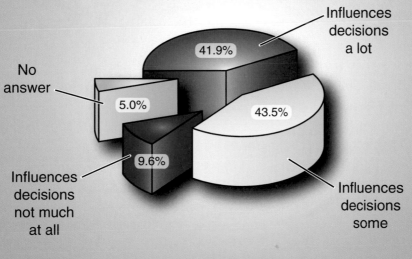

Public Believes Judges Are Partisan

Do you believe the partisan backgrounds of judges influence their court decisions?

Influences decisions a lot

41.9%

No answer

5.0%

43.5%

9.6%

Influences decisions not much at all

Influences decisions some

Taken from: Maxwell School, Syracuse University, Fall 2005 poll.

elected also, and their views on this sort of thing may be known as well. True, the Justices are not regularly held accountable in the way legislators are, but, as we have already remarked, we are not looking for perfection.

So, the defender of judicial review is not altogether tongue-tied in response to our citizen's challenge; there is something to say. Nevertheless, if legitimacy is a comparative matter, then it is a staggeringly inadequate response. The system of legislative elections is not perfect either, but it is evidently superior as a matter of democracy and democratic values to the indirect and limited basis of democratic legitimacy for the judiciary. Legislators are regularly accountable to their constituents and they behave as though their electoral credentials were important in relation to the overall ethos of their participation in political decisionmaking. None of this is true of Justices.

Justices Don't Represent Anyone

Second, even if we concede that vexed issues of rights should be decided by these nine men and women, why should they be decided by simple majority voting among the Justices? Here, the situation gets worse for defenders of judicial review. I have always been intrigued by the fact that courts make their decisions by voting, applying the MD [majority decision] principle to their meager numbers. I know they produce reasons. . . . But in the end it comes down to head-counting: five votes defeat four in the U.S. Supreme Court, irrespective of the arguments that the Justices have concocted. If MD is challenged in this context, can we respond to it in roughly the same way that we imagined a response on behalf of legislatures? Actually, no, we cannot. MD is appropriate for persons who have a moral claim to insist on being regarded as equals in some decision-process. But I cannot see any moral basis for this claim in the case of Supreme Court Justices. They do not represent anybody. Their claim to participate is functional, not a matter of entitlement.

I am handicapped here by the more or less complete lack of theoretical attention to the use of MD in courts. Scholars have written some about our empirical experience of voting and voting strategy on courts, and some have suggested novel ways of combining judges' votes on the particular issues involved in each case, rather than on the overall outcome. But I am not aware of any elementary defense of judicial majoritarianism. The usual fairness-and-equality defense is unavailable. I suspect that if the use of MD by courts were to be defended, it would be defended either as a simple technical device of decision with no further theoretical ramifications, or on the basis of [the eighteenth-century Marquis de] Condorcet's jury theorem (majority voting by a group of adjudicators arithmetically enhances the competence of the group beyond the average competence of its members). If it is the latter, then the defense of MD is part of the outcome-related case for judicial competence, which means that it will have to compete with a similar case that can be made for the much larger voting bodies in legislatures. However this argument would play out, my point is this: There is no additional fairness argument for the use of MD by courts, as there is for its use by legislatures.

Judicial Review Undemocratic

These last points should remind us that the responses we have been imagining to [a citizen's] challenge to legislative and judicial procedures do not stand alone. . . .

The reasons on both sides have to do with rights. If one institution or the other was clearly superior at determining what rights people really have, then that would weigh very heavily indeed in favor of that institution. But that is not the case. On the process side, institutions giving final authority on these matters to judges fail to offer any sort of adequate response to the fairness-complaint of the ordinary citizen based on the principle—not just the value—of political equality. That failure might be tolerable if there were a convincing outcome-based

Visitors to the Supreme Court's opening session wait in line for the first session of the court term. Some people believe that appointed judges should not be allowed to judge on constitutional measures because their own opinions may not match what the public would choose.

case for judicial decisionmaking. Defenders of judicial review pretend that there is. But . . . it is just unsupported assertion.

Perhaps aware of all this, defenders of judicial review have tried a number of last-ditch attempts to reconcile their favored institution to democratic values. . . .

Judges Define Our Rights

Defenders of judicial review claim that judges are simply enforcing the society's own precommitment to rights. The society has bound itself to the mast on certain principles of right, and, like Ulysses' shipmates, the judges are just making sure the ropes remain tied. This common analogy has been thoroughly discredited in the literature. Briefly, the response is that the society has not committed itself to any particular view of what a given right entails, so when citizens disagree about this, it is not clear why giving judges the power to decide should be understood as upholding a precommitment. . . .

Defenders of judicial review claim that if legislators disagree with a judicial decision about rights, they can campaign to amend the Bill of Rights to explicitly override it. Their failure to do this amounts to a tacit democratic endorsement. This argument is flawed because it does not defend the baseline that judicial decisionmaking establishes. Amending a Bill of Rights characteristically involves a supermajority; or if it is a British- or New Zealand-style statute, it will have credentials in the political culture that raise the stakes and increase the burden associated with the amendment effort. If our disgruntled citizen . . . asks why the deck should be stacked in this way, the only answer we can give her refers back to judicial decision. And that has already been found wanting. . . .

Judicial Review Undermines Political Equality

Defenders of judicial review insist that judges have democratic credentials: They are nominated and confirmed by elected officials, and the kind of judicial nominations that a candidate for political office is likely to make nowadays plays an important role in the candidate's electoral campaign. This is true; but (as I have already remarked) the issue is comparative, and these credentials are not remotely competitive with the democratic credentials of elected legislators. Moreover, to the extent that we accept judges because of their democratic credentials, we undermine the affirmative case that is made in favor of judicial review as a distinctively valuable form of political decisionmaking.

Fifth and finally, defenders of judicial review claim that the practice may be justified as an additional mode of access for citizen input into the political system. Sometimes citizens access the system as voters, sometimes as lobbyists, sometimes as litigants. They say we should evaluate the legitimacy of the whole package of various modes of citizen access, not just the democratic credentials of this particular component. The point is a fair one, as far as it goes. But embedding judicial review in a wider array of modes of citizen participation does not alter the fact that this is a mode of citizen involvement that is undisciplined by the principles of political equality usually thought crucial to democracy. People tend to look to judicial review when they want greater weight for their opinions than electoral politics would give them.

EVALUATING THE AUTHOR'S ARGUMENTS:

The author criticizes judicial review as undemocratic. Does he suggest an alternative method of interpreting the constitution? Whom would you trust more to interpret the constitution, judges or legislators? Why?

Courts Should Have the Power of Judicial Review

Scott Gerber

"Judicial review is . . . the federal judiciary's only significant check on the power of Congress, the president, the states . . . and the people themselves."

Scott Gerber argues in the following viewpoint that the U.S. Constitution creates an independent judiciary whose main purpose is to protect individual rights. Claims that judicial review is undemocratic are misleading, he contends, because our government is that of a republic rather than of a democracy. Judicial review is part of the checks and balances political theory relied upon by the Founders when creating our Constitution. Gerber is a senior research scholar in law and politics at the Social Philosophy and Policy Center at Bowling Green State University in Ohio.

AS YOU READ, CONSIDER THE FOLLOWING QUESTIONS:

1. What Supreme Court justice quoted by the author called for appointment of justices based wholly on functional fitness?

2. Why does Gerber think lifetime appointments of justices is necessary for an independent judiciary?
3. In the author's summary of the political theory upon which judicial review is based, what was the purpose of dividing power among the legislative, executive, and judicial branches?

It's probably fair to say that only law professors themselves know, and care, about most . . . policy debates in the nation's law schools. However, there is a major debate currently underway that those who work outside of the ivory tower should care about, and probably don't know about.

It's the debate over whether judicial review in the United States should be eliminated, or at least drastically curtailed. . . .

Attacking Judicial Review

For readers who haven't revisited *Marbury v. Madison* (1803) since their law school days, judicial review may be defined as the power of a court to hold unconstitutional and hence unenforceable any law, any official action based on a law, or any other action by a public official deemed in conflict with the Constitution of the United States.

Professor Cass R. Sunstein of the University of Chicago Law School and Professor Mark V. Tushnet of Harvard Law School insist that judicial review is bad policy. Dean Larry D. Kramer of Stanford Law School and Dean William M. Treanor of Fordham Law School maintain that judicial review, at least as practiced and understood by the modern federal judiciary, is without historical foundation. And Professor Jeremy Waldron of New York University School of Law claims it's philosophically indefensible. . . .

U.S. Is a Republic Not a Democracy

I'll start with Professor Waldron's philosophical argument. Admittedly, I'm no philosopher, but history and political science make plain that the Constitution establishes a republic, not a democracy. In a republic, decisionmakers are elected—or, in the federal judiciary's case, appointed by those who are elected—to govern the polity. Consequently, Professor Waldron's "core case" against judicial review is issued against a straw man. Or, as a philosopher might put it, his "core case" is based on an "invalid premise" about the nature of the American constitutional order.

Moreover, the fact that federal judges have the time and job security to be philosophers suggests that a philosopher such as Professor Waldron should favor, rather than oppose, judicial review. In a famous 1957 essay calling for the appointment of Supreme Court justices "wholly on the basis of functional fitness," [Supreme Court Justice] Felix Frankfurter made a similar point.

Judiciary Exists to Protect Rights, Not Promote Policy

With respect to the policy arguments against judicial review proffered by Professors Sunstein and Tushnet, policy is like beauty: it lies in the eye of the beholder. What might seem like good policy to them, might seem like bad policy to some of the rest of us. Professor Burt Neuborne of New York University School of Law put it well in a review of another of Professor Sunstein's books, *Democracy and the Problem of Free Speech*: "[M]any of Professor Sunstein's distinctions lack a principled basis, other than Cass Sunstein's own view of what should or should not be censored. . . . In the end, his argument comes down to allowing [his] social class to use the government to elevate its speech preferences over everyone else's."

The same may be said of Professor Tushnet's policy arguments. An article in *Dissent* magazine that previewed a key chapter of Professor Tushnet's anti-judicial review book was entitled "Is Judicial Review Good for the Left?" As someone who thinks that most of the policies promoted by the left are unwise, I hope the answer to that question is "no." And if the answer is, in fact, "no," then as a policy matter I'm strongly in favor of judicial review.

However, whether I—or Professors Tushnet or Sunstein—think judicial review is good (or bad) policy should be irrelevant in a regime such as ours, dedicated as the United States is supposed to be to the rule of law. History makes plain that the U.S. Constitution establishes an independent judiciary whose principal purpose is to protect individual rights. Dean Kramer's and Dean Treanor's arguments to the contrary are therefore incorrect.

Founders Intended Independent Judiciary

Dean Kramer devotes virtually his entire book to describing episodes in American history in which he claims the people, rather than the judiciary, defined what the Constitution meant. Dean Treanor dedicate the entirety of his law review article to the cases that anticipated *Marbury*. What both fail to address, then, is the political theory that made judicial review possible, and that helps to explain why we need it. As I put it in the political theory chapter of a book I'm writing on the origins of an independent judiciary, that political theory—in summary form—is this:

> It all began with Aristotle's theory of a mixed constitution, a theory that divided government into three parts, with each part representing a political class of the regime. Next came Polybius, who emphasized the checking and balancing of government power, albeit power still divided along class, rather than institutional, lines. Marsilius of Padua was the initial political theorist to focus on the function of particular institutions, while Sir John Fortescue was the first to appreciate the unique role of the judiciary. Gasparo Contarini was responsible for marrying the Aristotelian theory of mixed government to the concept of checks and balances, and Charles I took the pivotal step of committing Anglo-American constitutional theory to the notion of balance among political institutions, rather than dominance by one. Montesquieu contributed the most famous idea of all: that political power should be divided among the legislative, executive, and judicial branches of government so as to ensure the people's liberty. Finally, John Adams argued that judges, and not simply temporary juries (as Montesquieu had argued), need to be independent from the executive and legislative branches, and that this would be possible only if judges were afforded life tenure during good behavior and paid adequate and stable salaries.

The foundation of the government, and its relation to the constitution, relies on its roots as a republic instead of a democracy.

Judicial Review Preserves Individual Rights

In short, although political architecture is not solely the provenance of political theorists, it was political theory that led America's constitutional framers to use the lessons of history to create a judicial branch whose independence plays such an essential role in the preservation of individual rights. Judicial review is, of course, the ultimate expression of judicial independence—no judge without secure tenure and a salary that can't be diminished would dare to invalidate the decisions of the political actors who control his or her livelihood—and it represents the federal judiciary's only significant check on the power of Congress, the president, the states . . . and the people themselves.

Legal academics who question the legitimacy of judicial review ignore political theory at their peril.

The Executive Power Should Be Reduced

Al Gore

"As a result of its unprecedented claim of new unilateral power, the Executive Branch has now put our constitutional design at grave risk."

In the following excerpts from a speech given at Constitution Hall on January 16, 2006, Al Gore argues that the executive branch has claimed broad powers not granted by the Constitution. Gore claims that along with efforts to increase executive power, judicial power and legislative power have been weakened, creating a dangerous imbalance of power among the three branches of government that threatens the future of democracy. Gore was vice president of the United States from 1993 to 2001.

AS YOU READ, CONSIDER THE FOLLOWING QUESTIONS:
1. Quoting Thomas Paine, who or what does the author say was intended to be "king" in America?
2. What, according to Gore, has historically been the principal alternative to democracy?

3. Whom does the author blame for the failure of checks and balances to prevent excessive executive power?

Many of us have come here to Constitution Hall to sound an alarm and call upon our fellow citizens to put aside partisan differences and join with us in demanding that our Constitution be defended and preserved. . . .

[In December 2005], Americans awoke to the shocking news that in spite of this long settled law, the Executive Branch has been secretly spying on large numbers of Americans . . . and eavesdropping on "large volumes of telephone calls, e-mail messages, and other Internet traffic inside the United States." The *New York Times* reported that the President decided to launch this massive eavesdropping program "without search warrants or any new laws that would permit such domestic intelligence collection."

During the period when this eavesdropping was still secret, the President went out of his way to reassure the American people on more than one occasion that, of course, judicial permission is required for any government spying on American citizens and that, of course, these constitutional safeguards were still in place. But surprisingly, the President's soothing statements turned out to be false. Moreover, as soon as this massive domestic spying program was uncovered by the press, the President not only confirmed that the story was true, but also declared that he has no intention of bringing these wholesale invasions of privacy to an end. . . .

Law Should Be King

A president who breaks the law is a threat to the very structure of our government. Our Founding Fathers were adamant that they had established a government of laws and not men. Indeed, they recognized that the structure of government they had enshrined in our Constitution— our system of checks and balances—was designed with a central purpose of ensuring that it would govern through the rule of law. As John Adams said: "The executive shall never exercise the legislative and judicial powers, or either of them, to the end that it may be a government of laws and not of men."

An executive who arrogates to himself the power to ignore the legitimate legislative directives of the Congress or to act free of the check of the judiciary becomes the central threat that the Founders sought to nullify in the Constitution—an all-powerful executive too reminiscent of the King from whom they had broken free. In the words of James Madison, "the accumulation of all powers, legislative, executive, and judiciary, in the same hands, whether of one, a few, or many, and whether hereditary, self-appointed, or elective, may justly be pronounced the very definition of tyranny."

Thomas Paine, whose pamphlet, "On Common Sense" ignited the American Revolution, succinctly described America's alternative. Here, he said, we intended to make certain that "the law is king."...

Once violated, the rule of law is in danger. Unless stopped, lawlessness grows. The greater the power of the executive grows, the more difficult it becomes for the other branches to perform their constitutional roles. As the executive acts outside its constitutionally prescribed role and is able to control access to information that would expose its actions, it becomes increasingly difficult for the other branches to

The balance between executive, judicial, and legislative power has, in many people's opinions, been unbalanced by the increase in executive decisions.

police it. Once that ability is lost, democracy itself is threatened and we become a government of men and not laws. . . .

Claims of New Powers

The President has also declared that he has a heretofore unrecognized inherent power to seize and imprison any American citizen that he alone determines to be a threat to our nation, and that, notwithstanding his American citizenship, the person imprisoned has no right to talk with a lawyer—even to argue that the President or his appointees have made a mistake and imprisoned the wrong person.

The President claims that he can imprison American citizens indefinitely for the rest of their lives without an arrest warrant, without notifying them about what charges have been filed against them, and without informing their families that they have been imprisoned.

At the same time, the Executive Branch has claimed a previously unrecognized authority to mistreat prisoners in its custody in ways that plainly constitute torture in a pattern that has now been documented in U.S. facilities located in several countries around the world. . . .

The President has also claimed that he has the authority to kidnap individuals in foreign countries and deliver them for imprisonment and interrogation on our behalf by autocratic regimes in nations that are infamous for the cruelty of their techniques for torture. . . . Can it be true that any president really has such powers under our Constitution? If the answer is "yes" then under the theory by which these acts are committed, are there any acts that can on their face be prohibited? If the President has the inherent authority to eavesdrop, imprison citizens on his own declaration, kidnap and torture, then what can't he do?. ..

Need for Checks and Balances

As a result of its unprecedented claim of new unilateral power, the Executive Branch has now put our constitutional design at grave risk. The stakes for America's representative democracy are far higher than has been generally recognized.

These claims must be rejected and a healthy balance of power restored to our Republic. Otherwise, the fundamental nature of our democracy may well undergo a radical transformation.

For more than two centuries, America's freedoms have been preserved in part by our founders' wise decision to separate the aggregate power of our government into three co-equal branches, each of which serves to check and balance the power of the other two. . . .

The principal alternative to democracy throughout history has been the consolidation of virtually all state power in the hands of a single strongman or small group who together exercise that power without the informed consent of the governed.

It was in revolt against just such a regime, after all, that America was founded. . . .

Unilateral Executive

[The George W. Bush] Administration has come to power in the thrall of a legal theory that aims to convince us that this excessive concentration of presidential authority is exactly what our Constitution intended.

This legal theory, which its proponents call the theory of the unitary executive but which is more accurately described as the unilateral executive, threatens to expand the president's powers until the contours of the constitution that the Framers actually gave us become obliterated beyond all recognition. Under this theory, the President's authority when acting as Commander-in-Chief or when making foreign policy cannot be reviewed by the judiciary or checked by Congress. President Bush has pushed the implications of this idea to its maximum by continually stressing his role as Commander-in-Chief, invoking it has frequently as he can, conflating it with his other roles, domestic and foreign. When added to the idea that we have entered a perpetual state of war, the implications of this theory stretch quite literally as far into the future as we can imagine. . . .

A Weakened Judiciary

In a properly functioning system, the Judicial Branch would serve as the constitutional umpire to ensure that the branches of government observed their proper spheres of authority, observed civil liberties and adhered to the rule of law. Unfortunately, the unilateral executive has tried hard to thwart the ability of the judiciary to call balls and strikes by keeping controversies out of its hands—notably those challenging its ability to detain individuals without legal process—by appointing judges who will be deferential to its exercise of power and by its support of assaults on the independence of the third branch. . . .

The Administration has supported the assault on judicial independence that has been conducted largely in Congress. That assault includes a threat by the Republican majority in the Senate to permanently change the rules to eliminate the right of the minority to engage in extended debate of the President's judicial nominees. The assault has extended to legislative efforts to curtail the jurisdiction of courts in matters ranging from *habeas corpus* to the pledge of allegiance. In short, the Administration has demonstrated its contempt for the judicial role and sought to evade judicial review of its actions at every turn.

A Weakened Legislative Branch

But the most serious damage has been done to the legislative branch. The sharp decline of congressional power and autonomy in recent years has been almost as shocking as the efforts by the Executive Branch to attain a massive expansion of its power. . . .

It is the pitiful state of our legislative branch which primarily explains the failure of our vaunted checks and balances to prevent the dangerous overreach by our Executive Branch which now threatens a radical transformation of the American system.

I call upon Democratic and Republican members of Congress today to uphold your oath of office and defend the Constitution. Stop going along to get along. Start acting like the independent and co-equal branch of government you're supposed to be.

EVALUATING THE AUTHOR'S ARGUMENTS:

The author says that the executive branch claims that the president's actions as commander in chief or when making foreign policy cannot be reviewed by the judiciary or checked by Congress. If that were true, do you think that would be good or bad? Give reasons for your answer.

The Executive Power Should Not Be Reduced

David B. Rivkin Jr.

David B. Rivkin Jr. argues in the following viewpoint that the Constitution vests all executive power in the President. The Founders did this, he says, because they believed, based upon prior experience, that discretionary power could only be effectively wielded by a strong executive. Rivkin also argues that Congressional oversight or judicial review of the exercise of executive power violates separation of powers. Rivkin served in the Justice Department during the Ronald Reagan and George H.W. Bush administrations.

"The Framers created a strong president to ensure a strong national government that could protect the national interest."

AS YOU READ, CONSIDER THE FOLLOWING QUESTIONS:
1. What are two legitimate constitutional checks on executive power, according to the author?
2. Quoting Alexander Hamilton, what does Rivkin say is the result of a feeble executive?

David B. Rivkin Jr., "Enfeebling the Presidency: The Executive Branch is a Co-Equal Branch, or So the Framers Said," *National Review*, June 19, 2006. Copyright © 2006 by National Review, Inc., 215 Lexington Avenue, New York, NY 10016. Reproduced by permission.

D isputes over the nature and extent of presidential power are nothing new. Americans have fought about presidents, and the presidency, since the Republic's founding. The difference today is the vigor with which the institution itself, rather than simply the incumbent, is attacked, the comprehensive nature of the anti-executive sentiments, and the prevalence of these attacks on one side of the political spectrum. In particular, these attacks have taken three basic forms: 1) a basic denial of the president's role as the ultimate repository of all executive power—a principle sometimes referred to as the "unitary executive"; 2) the promotion of a model of executive power that would treat the president as little more than the executor of Congress's will, rather than an independent and co-equal branch of government; and, most especially, 3) demands that the courts serve a supervisory role over presidential decision-making—even with respect to the president's conduct of armed conflict. Only the last of these points is really new in American political discourse; but all are equally pernicious. . . .

Unitary Executive

Whether the entire executive power should be vested in a single elected official was one of the key questions considered by the 1787 Constitutional Convention. The fear, expressed over and over by various Framers, was that a single executive would tend inevitably toward monarchy. According to James Madison's *Notes of Debates in the Federal Convention*, Virginia's Edmund Randolph "strenuously opposed a unity in the Executive magistracy. He regarded it as the foetus of monarchy." Ultimately, however, that position did not carry the day: Although a single individual vested with all of the executive power—rather than several executive officers or a disposition of exec-utive functions among other branches of government—might look like a form of elected monarch, such a figure was essential to achiev-ing the unity of command, energy, and dispatch needed to defend the nation's interests. As Alexander Hamilton wrote in the *Federalist*:

Nearly Half of People Surveyed Believe President Can Suspend Constitution

Statement	Total Agreeing with Statement
The President can suspend the Constitution	**43%**
The President can suspend the constitutional freedoms of people like you anytime the President thinks it is necessary to protect the country.	18%
The President can suspend the constitutional freedoms of people like you only when authorized by a court of law or Congress.	25%
The President alone should never be able to suspend the constitutional freedoms of people like you.	**52%**
Don't know/Not sure	**3%**
Decline to answer	**2%**

Taken from: American Bar Association, February 7, 2006.

"Energy in the executive is a leading character in the definition of good government. . . . A feeble executive implies a feeble execution of the government. A feeble execution is but another phrase for a bad execution." In other words, the Framers adopted a unitary executive for good and sufficient reason: Achieving these ends had been the very purpose of drafting and adopting a new Constitution, reflecting the widespread dissatisfaction with the experience of our national governance under the Articles of Confederation, when the executive power was vested in Congress.

Thus, when . . . the *New York Times* characterized the unitary executive as a "fringe" theory, it was dismissing the actual intent and purpose of the Constitution's Framers—not to mention the plain meaning of that document's text, which states that "[t]he executive Power shall be vested in a President of the United States.". . . .

Congress Should Not Control Executive Branch

There is little doubt that the *Times* was trying to advance the broader view of the intellectual Left that there is effectively no power held by the president that should not be subject to the control of Congress and/or the courts. They do not believe that the president should merely be subject to actual constitutional checks and balances (such as impeachment or the power of the purse)—but that Congress and the courts have a right to direct on an ongoing basis how the president executes the core functions of his office.

Acceptance of this position would, of course, transform the presidency from a co-equal and independent branch of government into the servant of (chiefly) Congress. This is not what the Constitution provides for, and it was only a minority of that document's Framers who ever considered such an arrangement desirable. First among these was Connecticut's Roger Sherman. According to Madison's *Notes*, early in the Convention, when the delegates began discussion of the executive power, Sherman "said he considered the Executive magistracy as nothing more than an institution for carrying the will of the Legislature into effect." Again, as with opposition to a unitary executive, this position did not prevail. Indeed, much of the Convention's subsequent discussions revolved around how to ensure that the national executive would be independent of Congress. As Madison later wrote, the executive, legislative, and judicial powers must be both separate and "independent of each other. . . . Experience had proved a tendency in our governments to throw all power into the Legislative vortex. The Executives of the States are in general little more than Cyphers; the legislatures omnipotent. If no effectual check be devised for restraining the instability & encroachments of the latter, a revolution of some kind or other would be inevitable.". . .

Executive Must Have Discretion

As clearly understood by the Framers (inspired by such political philosophers as Montesquieu), discretionary governmental power can be properly wielded only by an executive. And, while any discretionary exercise of power can lead to abuses, the primary constitutional way to deal with this problem is through political accountability—not by having either Congress or the courts share in the decision-making process. One key part of this inherent executive discretion is the determination of who is, and who is not, an enemy combatant subject to attack and capture by American and allied forces in wartime. Although, as [U.S. Supreme Court] Justice [Clarence] Thomas noted, the question of whether "[a detainee]'s executive detention is lawful is a question properly resolved by the Judicial Branch . . . whether [the detainee] is actually an enemy combatant is [a determination] 'of a kind for which the Judiciary has neither aptitude, facilities nor responsibility and which has long been held to belong in the domain of political power not subject to judicial intrusion or inquiry.'"

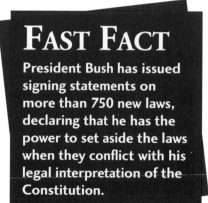

Executive Powers Are Legal

This has, in fact, long been the settled rule of constitutional jurisprudence. Unfortunately, in 2004, Justice Thomas was writing in dissent, the majority of justices having agreed that some form of process—albeit one formulated and administered by the executive— was required to permit detainees to challenge their classification as "enemy combatants." Still, even this was not sufficient for many of the administration's critics, who continued to deny the legitimacy of these detentions in the absence of a full criminal trial.

Similarly, arguments have been made that the president's interpretation of the Geneva Conventions with respect to the conflict with al-Qaeda and the Taliban should be subject to judicial revision. The courts do, of course, interpret and apply treaties in those instances where the justiciable rights of individuals are involved. In a case like the Geneva Conventions, however, where the "rights" are held by nations—e.g., the U.S. has a right to have its captured soldiers treated as "prisoners of war" under the Third Geneva Convention—and not by individuals, it is up to the executive to construe and apply U.S. treaty obligations.

Congress is believed by some to have equal authority to the other branches of government.

Most recently, of course, the entire controversy over the National Security Agency's program to intercept al-Qaeda communications into and out of the U.S. has involved claims that the president violated the 1978 Foreign Intelligence Surveillance Act (FISA), and that all such surveillance decisions must be subject to judicial approval or disapproval. It has long been recognized that the president has the inherent constitutional right, as chief executive and commander-in-chief, to conduct warrantless surveillance for national-security purposes, both at home and abroad. This authority has been affirmed by those courts that have discussed the question. . . .

Courts Should Not Supervise Executive

It is difficult to imagine a more effective means of ensuring that the president will not act decisively than involving the courts in supervising his actions. Courts are, by nature, deliberative, and deliberation takes time. The courts have little or no means of obtaining and analyzing the information necessary to make foreign or military policy; they are not cohesive (various trial and appellate courts issue inconsistent decisions on the same subjects, and the Supreme Court often has real trouble ensuring that lower courts follow its lead); they cannot execute their own orders; and they do not command the public's confidence or affection as a president can in times of crisis. They have, however, a long and proven record of advancing "progressive" causes, and many on the left continue to assume that the courts will provide more such results than could be expected from the political process.

Those conservatives who, out of anger or disappointment, wish to see the Bush administration bridled, or who fear that the power claimed by President Bush today will be used for worse ends by a Democratic successor tomorrow, should keep in mind Hamilton's words quoted above: "A feeble executive implies a feeble execution of the government. A feeble execution is but another phrase for a bad execution." The Framers created a strong president to ensure a strong national government that could protect the national interest. That concern remains as central today as it was in 1787.

Mayors Should Have More Power

Viewpoint 5

Richard C. Schragger

"The strong mayoralty is a potential instrument for demo-cratic self-government"

Richard C. Schragger argues in the following viewpoint that laws on the local level give mayors little power. Schragger contends that among local government institutions the office of mayor is best suited to assert power effectively. Mayors should be more than city managers or "technocrats," he maintains, because mayors can best represent the interests of the city as a whole in a system of federalism that, Schragger concludes, devalues the city power compared with that of state and federal power. Schragger is a professor of law at the University of Virginia.

AS YOU READ, CONSIDER THE FOLLOWING QUESTIONS:
1. In what size cities does the office of mayor mostly tend to be merely a ceremonial office, according to the author?
2. According to Frederic Howe, as quoted by Schragger, what has dictated most city laws?
3. What does the author think about traditional skepticism of local executive power?

The mayoralty's weakness has two grounds. First, the office's lack of power is a product of elite skepticism of urban democracy. That skepticism manifested itself in Progressive Era reforms that almost entirely eliminated the mayor's office in favor of a city council and professional city manager; the mayoralty continues to be a ceremonial office in most small- and medium-sized cities. Second, the mayoralty's weakness is a result of a federal system that devalues city—and, by extension, mayoral—power. American-style federalism privileges regional governments rather than local ones; states, not cities, are the salient sites for constitutionally protected "local" governance. This

It is widely disputed that mayors of cities, even major ones like New York City's Rudy Giuliani, are merely figureheads to enforce laws passed down from state and federal authority.

structural fact has political consequences. The city's limited capacity to make effective policy reinforces the parochialism of its leaders; their parochialism, in turn, reinforces the city's subordinate status. The challenge for urban reformers is to alter this "constitutional" weakness of the mayoralty. I argue that the strong mayoralty is a potential instrument for democratic self-government to the extent that it is able to amass power on behalf of the city. . . .

The mayoralty . . . has the institutional capacity to represent the city as a city, with identifiable interests independent of the preferences of any particular agglomeration of competing interest groups. That does not mean that the mayor will always (or usually) pursue the city's interests; the mayor's office is obviously responsive to particularist interests and is susceptible to their capture. Nevertheless, as with the presidency, executive power is most legitimate and arguably most effective when it is invoked on behalf of the entire polity. This characteristic of the executive makes the mayoralty a better candidate than other city institutions for asserting power within a political system that tends systematically to disadvantage cities.

Strong Mayors Can Embody City's Interests

The democratic argument for the strong mayor is thus not grounded in a pluralist account of urban politics, but rather in an older tradition, which some might call "civic republican." That tradition, derived from the ancients, views the city as the embodiment of the democratic polity (and not merely a reflection of the individuals or groups within it). Those who see the city solely as a political space in which interests or groups compete for domination or influence, as the pluralist or elite conceptions of urban politics would have it, tend to be skeptical of any concentration of political power. But if one views the city as a polity with a collective identity and interests independent of the particular ends of the citizens who inhabit it, then the embodiment of those interests in one executive office becomes more attractive. The articulation of the city's interests by a single executive official is particularly important for urban municipalities, which experience the most significant gaps between resources and responsibilities. . . .

Because of the limitations on the city council and other local political structures, the mayor's office is more likely to be able to assert local democratic prerogatives in a way that challenges the political subservience of the city more generally. In this way, a strong mayoralty derived from a democratic vision of city power is more likely to have substantial effects on city power than one derived from a technocratic understanding of the city and the mayor's role. . . .

Mistrust of Local Power

The weakness of the mayoralty illustrates a number of features of American political organization: the elite skepticism of democracy, a belief in technocracy as a solution to political failures, an emphasis on legal decentralization over political decentralization, and a federal system that fractures local power. More so than the presidency or the governorship, the mayoralty was shaped by an abiding ambivalence about the exercise of political power. Municipal policymakers came to believe the professionalization of city management would do more to promote city efficiency than its politicization. As [government reformer] Frederic Howe, a dissenter from this strategy, wrote, "Distrust of democracy has inspired much of the literature on the city. Distrust of democracy has dictated most of our city laws. . . . Reform organizations have voted democracy a failure."

FAST FACT

Nearly 20 percent of mayors in cities of thirty thousand people or more are women.

Distrust of urban democratic power remains apparent today in the dominance of the divided executive—the features of most city governments prove that we have internalized this suspicion. The professional manager provides a comforting image of governance in which executive power—in fact, the exercise of political power of any kind—is submerged and repressed. Weak-mayor charters and the dominance of the council-manager model reflect the widespread notion that municipal government is mainly administrative in nature. This understanding indirectly serves the interests of mayors' political competitors at the state and federal level, who benefit from mayors' lack of power. The ideology of municipal technocracy both cabins city power and enhances the power of those at higher levels of government.

Cities Need a Capacity to Respond

In an era in which state and national governments are retreating from a serious urban policy or a social welfarist agenda, cities have to increase their capacity to respond to both the substantive and the participatory demands of their constituents. Though efficiency and democracy are often conceptually at odds, executive power has recently been viewed as a way to move forward along both dimensions. This view, which seems unremarkable at the national level, has been repressed at the municipal level. In part because of the long-running association of municipal politics with the political machine, strength in the executive seems most threatening in municipalities. But the city is directly accountable and accessible to the citizenry in ways that other levels of government are not. Indeed, the mayor contends most directly with citizens' dissatisfaction with government failures even if those failures are entirely outside her control. For that reason alone, the traditional skepticism of local executive power should be reevaluated. . . .

But the city's weakness (and the mayor's) is also a product of our constitutional design—of the city's institutional subordination and fragmentation.

Current strong-mayor reforms address only one aspect of the fragmentation of the democratic city. They do little to challenge the city's constitutional subordination. And to the extent that strong-mayor charter reforms are grounded in a corporate or administrative model of local government, they are unlikely to alter intergovernmental relationships in the city's favor. Whether a strong mayoralty derived from democratic norms can alter those relationships is an open question. If cities are worth governing, however, the strong mayoralty in the democratic city may be worth a try.

EVALUATING THE AUTHOR'S ARGUMENTS:

The author emphasizes reasons for making mayors stronger. What are reasons for not doing so? Do you believe the pros outweigh the cons? Why or why not?

Chapter 3

How Should Government Function in the Future?

Many presidents have sought advice from prominent religious leaders.

Viewpoint

1

Government Can Help the People

Thom Hartmann

In the following viewpoint, Thom Hartmann contends that conservative leaders do not believe government can help people. Instead, he argues, they see government as a means of making money for themselves and their friends. This view is contrary, Hartmann says, to the Founding Fathers' view of the purpose of government. Hartmann maintains that when leaders use government to help people, as it did for the victims of Hurricane Charley in 2004, government works. Hartmann is a radio talk show host and author of *We the People* and other books about government.

"You can't govern if you don't believe in government."

AS YOU READ, CONSIDER THE FOLLOWING QUESTIONS:

1. Who began the dismantling of government, according to the author?
2. What clause in the preamble to the Constitution does Hartmann cite as proof that the Founders believed government was intended to help people?
3. Who, instead of government, does the author say conservatives believe should be in charge of nurturing, protecting, and defending individuals?

In a May 25, 2001 interview, [political thinker] Grover Norquist told National Public Radio's Mara Liasson, "I don't want to abolish government. I simply want to reduce it to the size where I can drag it into the bathroom and drown it in the bathtub."

Norquist got his wish. Democracy—and at least several thousand people, most of them Democrats, black, and poor—drowned in the basin of New Orleans [after flooding from hurricanes]. Our nation failed in its response, because for most of the past 25 years conservatives who don't believe in governance have run our government.

Destroying Government

As incompetent as George W. Bush has been in his response to the

Federal, state and local governments all pitched in when Hurricane Katrina devastated the Southern United States.

disaster in New Orleans, he wasn't the one who began the process that inevitably led to that disaster spiraling out of control.

That would be [former president] Ronald Reagan.

It was Reagan who began the deliberate and intentional destruction of the United States of America when he famously cracked (and then incessantly repeated): "The nine most terrifying words in the English language are, 'I'm from the government and I'm here to help.'"

Reagan, like George W. Bush after him, failed to understand that when people come together into community, and then into nationhood, that they organize themselves to protect themselves from predators, both human and corporate, both domestic and foreign. This form of organization is called government.

But the Reagan/Bush ideologues don't "believe" in government, in anything other than a military and police capacity. Government should punish, they agree, but it should never nurture, protect, or defend individuals. Nurturing and protecting, they suggest, is the more appropriate role of religious institutions, private charities, families, and—perhaps most important—corporations.

Let the corporations handle your old-age pension. Let the corporations decide how much protection we and our environment need from their toxics. Let the corporations decide what we're paid. Let the corporations decide what doctor we can see, when, and for what purpose.

Government Was Intended to Help People

This is the exact opposite of the vision for which the Founders of this nation fought and died. When Thomas Jefferson changed [English philosopher] John Locke's "Life, liberty, and private property" to "Live, liberty, and the pursuit of happiness," it was the first time in the history of the world that a newly founded nation had written the word "happiness" into its founding document. The phrase "promote the general welfare"—another revolutionary concept—first appeared in the preamble to our Constitution in 1787.

Talk show cons [conservatives] and TV talking head cons and political cons—both Republican and DLC [Democratic Leadership Council] Democratic—repeat the mantra of "smaller government," and Americans nod their heads in agreement, not realizing the hidden agenda at work.

Reagan was the first American president to actually preach that his own job was a bad thing. He once said, "Politics is supposed to be the second oldest profession. I have come to realize that it bears a very close resemblance to the first." One can only assume he was speaking of himself and his fellow Republicans, and certainly the current Congress's devotion to the interests of inherited wealth and large corporations displays how badly his philosophy has corrupted a role so noble it drew idealists like Jefferson, Lincoln, and the two Roosevelts.

Government and Self-Interest

But cons can't imagine anybody wanting to devote their lives to the service of their nation. The highest calling in their minds is to make profit.

As Reagan said: "The best minds are not in government. If any were, business would hire them away."

This mind-set—that the only purpose for service in government is to set up the interests of business—may account for why not a single military-eligible member of the Bush or Cheney families has enlisted in their parents' "Noble Cause," whereas all four sons of [former president] Franklin Roosevelt joined and each was decorated—on merit—for bravery in the deadly conflict of World War II.

There are, after all, no reasons in the conservative worldview for government service other than self-enrichment. As Ronald Reagan said: "Politics is not a bad profession. If you succeed there are many rewards, if you disgrace yourself you can always write a book."

FAST FACT

Nearly 26 million people a month received food stamps in 2005.

What they don't say is that the reason they want to remove government in its protective capacity is because they can then make an enormous amount of money, and have a lot of control over people's lives, when they privatize former governmental functions. They want a power vacuum, so corporations and the rich can step in. And with no limits on the inheritability of riches after the "death tax" is ended, wealth vast enough to take over the government can emerge. . . .

Proof Government Can Help

It's not that these conservatives are incompetent or stupid. When their interests are at stake, they can be very efficient. Consider when Hurricane Charley hit Jeb Bush's state—a year earlier than Katrina—on the second weekend of August, 2004, just months before the elections. . . .

In just the first thirteen days after Hurricane Charley hit Florida, the White House web site notes that the Bush administration had succeeded in:

—Registering approximately 136,000 assistance applicants
—Approving over 13,500 applications for more than $59 million in housing assistance
—Establishing 12 disaster recovery centers, which have assisted nearly 19,000 disaster victims
—Deploying medical teams that have seen nearly 3,000 patients
—Disbursing 1.2 million liters of water, 8.1 million pounds of ice, and 2 million meals and snacks
—Delivering over 20,000 rolls of plastic sheeting and nearly 170 generators
—Treating more than 2,900 individuals through FEMA [Federal Emergency Management Agency] Disaster Medical Assistance Teams, supporting damaged hospitals

Need to Believe in Government

That, of course, was for a Republican State, with a Republican governor, the crony brother of the President. Republicans needed to act like they cared about governing, because they wanted people to vote for them three months later.

But now, with no election looming and with death stalking a Democratic State [i.e., Louisiana] with a Democratic Governor unrelated to the President, we once again see the Reagan philosophy held ascendant. Bush's call to action? "Send cash to the Red Cross." One of those "thousand points of light" non-governmental organizations his father told us about.

As Brian Gurney, a [radio show] listener from California, noted: "You can't govern if you don't believe in government."

EVALUATING THE AUTHOR'S ARGUMENTS:

The author argues that government can help people. What are the pros and cons of relying on government, rather than on private individuals and charities, to help people? Give reasons for your answers.

Government Is Not Suited to Help the People

Bob Burg

Bob Burg argues in this viewpoint that government is ill-suited to care for the welfare of those in need. While a safety net is needed, historically, he says, this function was performed by charities, private civic groups, and religious organizations. The assumption that government is qualified to help the needy is, he says, a false premise. Burg argues that government's efforts to help those in need not only have failed, but have done more harm than good. Burg is a speaker and author on business topics.

"People help people. Governments don't help— they hurt."

AS YOU READ, CONSIDER THE FOLLOWING QUESTIONS:

1. How has government-sponsored welfare affected the number of homeless, according to the author?
2. According to the author, what percentage of tax dollars spent on welfare goes towards government bureaucracy?
3. How does the author characterize taxing one citizen in order to give benefits to another?

T he, term "Free-Market Advocate" should never be confused with "uncharitable," even though that's what many people who don't know better tend to think. Why is that?

Welfare State Is Wrong

Because free-market advocates don't believe in the welfare state—we don't believe that government has the right to forcibly pick the pocket of one person in order to give to another, regardless of how noble the intention might be. (The fact that government has never, in our two-hundred-year history, ever had any rights given—only powers "granted," conditionally— by its citizens, other than to protect them from force or fraud is a whole other article.)

And yes, without anger, I do use the term "pick the pocket" just to make the point that whether or not one calls it "theft" or "taxation," the results are the same. As the saying goes, "You can call an elephant a piano, but it still retains all the characteristics of an elephant."

"But Bob," the well-intended person will ask—often with incredulity that a person they know to otherwise be so charitable would feel so strongly about this—"if there is no taxation for welfare, what would happen to the poor person who cannot care for him or herself?"

And that, dear reader, is the crux of it: the reason and excuse for the multi-generational, hurtful, and anti-minority welfare state we "enjoy" today.

False Promise: That Government Can Help

The well-intentioned person who asks the question is worried about the poor, and this means two things:

1) This person is in fact a well-intentioned, caring human being who is disturbed by the fact that any of his fellow human beings ever have to suffer from poverty. Hopefully, we as free-market advocates also feel that same sympathy and empathy. It should distress us all that others have to suffer. I'd have to be concerned for anyone who doesn't feel that way, as one sign of a person's humanity is his ability to care about the situation of others and not just himself.

2) This person is basing his solution (government-forced, taxpayer-funded, or bureaucracy-imposed charity) on an extremely false and dangerous premise.

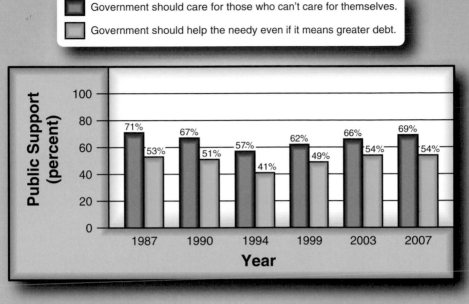

More Support for Government Programs

Surveys show an increase in public support for helping the poor .

■ Government should care for those who can't care for themselves.
□ Government should help the needy even if it means greater debt.

Taken from: Stephen Ohlemacher, Associated Press, February 26, 2007.

I'm not even talking here of the person's premise that says it's Constitutional for government to do this; it is not. The problem with that argument, however, is that he doesn't care. Our Constitution, at this point, has basically been discarded by those in Washington who swear to uphold and defend it. And even if this were not the case, to a kind, caring, compassion-minded person such as our friend, the end (helping the poor) would more than justify the means to do so anyway. So let's not even go with the "Constitution Argument."

Instead, let's discuss the false premise that government is in any way, shape, or form qualified to handle helping the truly needy.

Government Help Doesn't Work

Here's part of a recent discussion I had with a person who is disgusted with government and believes they should totally get out of our business:

Darlene (not her real name): Bob, don't you agree though, that there should be a safety net for the poor who cannot help themselves?

Me: Of course. I totally believe that.

Darlene: Then. . . ?

Me: What I don't believe, however, is that a bloated, wasteful, and otherwise incompetent (which she agreed with earlier) government is qualified to be the one to administer this "safety net." After all, they've been doing it for over 40 years now, and all that's been accomplished is. . .

I listed all the results of our government-sponsored and -applied welfare system, including the fact that we see more homeless and starving people now than we ever have before; that the separation between the haves and the have-nots is more pronounced than ever; that we've created a society of entitlement and robbed the welfare-dependent of any type of self-esteem they may ever have had, thereby keeping them down—not to mention the people who have "played" the system illegally.

She agreed this was so. I didn't even mention how much this costs the taxpayer due to the fact that about seventy percent of every forced tax dollar goes to pay the middle-class bureaucrats who actually have a vested interest in keeping the system going. They want to protect their jobs.

Darlene: But, if the government didn't do it, who would?

Okay, finally, we have the right question. And, still, the fact that it even has to be asked in the first place makes me sad. It reminds me that the people of this nation have forgotten how it was before government stepped in to replace a system that had worked much more effectively (not perfectly, but much, much better) than their own broken system.

FAST FACT

Nearly 1 in 6 people rely on some form of public assistance.

Let the Private Sector Do It

I explained that, in the days before government welfare, "people" took care of those less fortunate than they. This was done in a variety of ways: churches and synagogues, local charitable funds within munici-

As Senator Barack Obama speaks with doctors on a tour of a hospital, many wonder how government of any level can help with everyday concerns like health care.

palities where the poor lived, private contributions to various private charities, civic clubs, and organizations whose major role was to seek out those who were helpless and give them the financial lift they needed—this was just the tip of the iceberg of the help offered to the truly poor person and his family. (Important fact: While government-run programs typically see seventy percent of the funds go toward administration and salaries, and thirty percent to intended recipients, privately-run charities have the numbers reversed).

Even during The Depression (caused by government intervention in our money system, but that's another article), there were networks stretching across the nation that supplied needed funds, food, and other items to the needy. . . .

I'm a big proponent of the idea of "for-profit" charitable organizations, which would be ventures founded and run by entrepreneurs. They would solicit funds from individuals and companies in order to support one or more types of poor. The big differences between these organizations and the government-run ones would basically be:

1) The private, for-profit charity would be more accountable to its clients (donors), having to show them exact figures as to where the money would go, how it would be spent, and how much the organization would get to keep for their efforts. If they cheated and were caught, they would be held accountable, and perhaps face prison time, as opposed to the huge government bureaucracy backed by the full force (literally) and support of the government.

2) Since this private charity would be run by a businessperson with a profit motive, it would be run more efficiently. The fact is, a person running a private organization, who has a vested financial interest in its success, would run it much more efficiently than would bureaucrats who stand to make the same amount of money for not making changes and "messing up the works.

3) Since private taxpayers, by not having to pay into the present wasteful welfare system, will save thousands of dollars per year, they will have more disposable income to donate to these private, more efficient charities.

4) Those who are "playing the system" will have no source of "suckers" willing to give them money for free.

5) Those who are truly needy will see more charitable dollars and genuinely caring assistance than they ever have before. They will also be empowered and encouraged to help themselves to get off this privately-provided welfare and gain back their self-esteem; self-esteem they can now pass on to their descendants.

Is a "safety net" proper in a capitalist society? Once we redefine the term "safety net," I absolutely believe so. But remember: People help people. Governments don't help—they hurt. And even if their intentions are good, the results are not; and good intentions plus negative results does not equal positive results.

EVALUATING THE AUTHOR'S ARGUMENTS:

The author argues that the private sector rather than government should attend to the needy, and that there is a long tradition in the United States of private-sector organizations offering charitable services to the poor, elderly, and disabled. Do you believe that government welfare prevents the private sector from helping the needy even further? Discuss groups in the private sector that currently offer services to the needy.

Viewpoint

3

Religion Should Influence Political Decisions

Chris Kellerman

"Should our leaders make decisions based on their personal faith? They must."

In the following viewpoint, Chris Kellerman argues that political leaders should make decisions based on personal faith. He believes that commitment to religion is a promise to obey certain rules and requires political beliefs that conform to those rules. Americans, he contends, do not like politicians who claim to believe one thing but cast votes contrary to those beliefs. Politicians who live by a moral code, Kellerman maintains, necessarily must legislate in accordance with that code. Kellerman writes for Texas Technical University's student newspaper, the *Daily Toreador*.

AS YOU READ, CONSIDER THE FOLLOWING QUESTIONS:

1. According to the author, what religious group was largely responsible for the Republicans' success in elections in 2002 and 2004?

2. Why, in Kellerman's view, did the position of 2004 presidential candidate John Kerry on abortion cause voters to be suspicious of him?
3. In the author's opinion, how should Americans react if leaders don't let religious beliefs influence their decisions?

When John F. Kennedy ran for president in 1960, his critics warned that he would make too many of his decisions based on his Catholic faith, or that he would always seek counsel from the Vatican. These days, a Democrat criticized as "too religious" is a rare occurrence. The religious members of the Democratic Party in the past couple of decades have stopped speaking about God, while Christians in the Republican Party invoke his name regularly.

Democrats Now Embrace Religion

In 2000, Vice President Al Gore selected Joe Lieberman as his running mate, and the media called Gore's choice "groundbreaking" because Lieberman is an Orthodox Jew. Unfortunately, the media paid very little attention to how Lieberman's Judaism affected his policy decisions and instead focused only on the fact that America has never had a Jewish vice president.

Enter [George W. Bush's campaign architect] Karl Rove and the Bush White House. The 2002 and 2004 elections helped solidify a Republican majority in Congress largely due to a massive turnout of Evangelical voters. But in 2005, a strange thing happened in Virginia—Democrat Tim Kaine was elected governor. Kaine, a Catholic, did not shy away from discussing his religious beliefs on the campaign trail.

Suddenly, the Democratic Party realized it did not need to be afraid of religion. In 2006, more and more Democratic candidates turned their issues into moral issues, such as the Iraq war,

FAST FACT

A Pew Research Center poll found that 60 percent of white evangelicals surveyed believed the Bible should have more influence on the laws of the United States than the will of the American people.

Houses of Worship and Politics

Should houses of worship express views on politics?

	Keep Out (%)	Express Views (%)	Don't Know (%)
Total	46	51	3
July 2005	44	51	5
March 2001	43	51	6
June 1996	43	54	3
Feb 1968*	53	40	7
March 1957*	44	48	8
White	47	50	3
Black	35	62	3
18-29	43	54	3
30-49	42	56	2
50-64	49	48	3
65+	52	44	4
Conservative Republican	34	65	1
Mod/Lib Republican	49	48	3
Independent	48	49	3
Conserv/Mod Democrat	45	52	3
Liberal Democrat	59	38	3
East	53	44	3
Midwest	46	52	2
South	41	56	3
West	46	49	5
Total Protestant	39	58	3
White evangelical	34	63	3
White mainline	52	44	4
Black Protestant	29	68	3
Total Catholic	52	45	3
White, non-Hispanic	54	44	2
Secular	59	36	5

* 1957 and 1968 figures from Gallup

Taken from: The Pew Research Center, August 24, 2006.

health care and immigration. With that shift in message, a majority of religious voters cast their ballots for Democrats Nov. 7.

Leaders Must Decide Based on Faith

What does this mean for our country? Will religious people now only vote for Democrats? Of course not. It does mean, however, that the age-old debate has been resurrected: Is it okay for government and religion to intermingle? Should our leaders make decisions based on their personal faith? They must.

When Sen. John Kerry ran for president in 2004, he had the opposite problem as Kennedy. Most people found him to be a little shady when he would say that he was personally opposed to abortion because of his faith, but he did not think the government had the right to legislate it. I often heard friends say, "So wait, his faith teaches that abortion is murder, but he doesn't think that the government should legislate against murder?"

John Kerry lost. Americans do not like politicians who claim to believe one thing but have a record which proves otherwise, and rightfully so.

Personal beliefs, such as religion, play an important factor in the morality of court decisions.

Americans Like Religious Commitment

In fact, Americans should be horrified when leaders do not let their religious beliefs influence their decisions. To be a member of a religion is a serious matter. When a person decides which religion he will follow, he hopefully makes a commitment to follow any rules the religion may have and to instruct himself in the ways of that faith. Even religions with practically no dogma still ask their adherents to follow universally recognized moral guidelines.

So when a politician runs for office and says, "Oh, by the way, I'm a practicing (insert religion of choice here)," the public should be able to believe him. The public should also expect that a politician's political beliefs will not be entirely separate from his religious ones.

Separation of Church and State Is Irrelevant

Many people think politicians should disregard this philosophy because of the separation of church and state, but really, this issue has nothing to do with that. Let's open up our pocket Constitutions to the Bill of Rights and check out the First Amendment: "Congress shall make no law respecting an establishment of religion, or prohibiting the free exercise thereof." It is blatantly obvious that there is nothing in that clause which prohibits a politician from voting with his or her religious views.

Another criticism might be that politicians should not use their religious beliefs as guidelines for legislating because there are some people with controversial religious beliefs—for example, Islamic extremists. Here's an idea; don't vote for them. I would also hope atheist and agnostic voters would agree with me. Most of my non-religious friends try to live by a moral code of their own, and I think they vote along those principles in election booths, too.

Religion in Public Not Taboo

Unfortunately, we have to suffer through a period of watching politicians awkwardly tap their feet to gospel choirs and use troubling tactics to get religious voters to the polls. As to when the great day will come that the public forum is not a place where the discussion of religion is prohibited—God only knows.

EVALUATING THE AUTHOR'S ARGUMENTS:

Do you agree with the author's view that legislation should be dictated by religious beliefs? State arguments for and against such a view.

Viewpoint 4

Religion Should Not Influence Political Decisions

Sam Harris

"Infatuation with religious myths now poses a tremendous danger."

Sam Harris argues in the following viewpoint that irrational beliefs of religion harm politics. Religious dogma, he opines, impedes genuine wisdom and compassion. Religion separates questions of right and wrong from reality, resulting in domestic policies that cause suffering and a nihilism that undermines building a sustainable society, he maintains. Decisions about war and peace or domestic policy, the author contends, should be based on facts rather than on religious beliefs. Harris is an atheist and the author of *Letter to a Christian Nation.*

AS YOU READ, CONSIDER THE FOLLOWING QUESTIONS:
1. According to the author, what catastrophic event are half of Americans eagerly anticipating because of religious belief?
2. What did George W. Bush tell supporters of his presidential candidacy in 1999, according to Harris?
3. What is religion, in the author's view, not required to provide in support of its beliefs?

D espite a full century of scientific insights attesting to the antiquity of life and the greater antiquity of the Earth, more than half the American population believes that the entire cosmos was created 6,000 years ago. This is, incidentally, about a thousand years after the Sumerians invented glue. Those with the power to elect presidents and congressmen—and many who themselves get elected—believe that dinosaurs lived two by two upon Noah's Ark, that light from distant galaxies was created en route to the Earth and that the first members of our species were fashioned out of dirt and divine breath, in a garden with a talking snake, by the hand of an invisible God.

Americans Divided on Religion in Government

Who has gone too far?

	Conservative Christians in imposing their religious values	Liberals in keeping religion out of government
Total	49%	69%
Republican	31%	87%
Conservative	24%	90%
Moderate/Liberal	46%	82%
Democrat	59%	60%
Moderate/Conservative	51%	70%
Liberal	80%	38%
Independent	56%	65%

Taken from: The Pew Research Center, August 24, 2006.

Faith-Based Nihilism

This is embarrassing. But add to this comedy of false certainties the fact that 44 percent of Americans are confident that Jesus will return to Earth sometime in the next 50 years, and you will glimpse the terrible liability of this sort of thinking. Given the most common interpretation of Biblical prophecy, it is not an exaggeration to say that nearly half the American population is eagerly anticipating the end of the world. It should be clear that this faith-based nihilism provides its adherents with absolutely no incentive to build a sustainable civilization—economically, environmentally or geopolitically. Some of these people are lunatics, of course, but they are not the lunatic fringe. We are talking about the explicit views of Christian ministers who have congregations numbering in the tens of thousands. These are some of the most influential, politically connected and well-funded people in our society.

It is, of course, taboo to criticize a person's religious beliefs. The problem, however, is that much of what people believe in the name of religion is intrinsically divisive, unreasonable and incompatible with genuine morality. One of the worst things about religion is that it tends to separate questions of right and wrong from the living reality of human and animal suffering. Consequently, religious people will devote immense energy to so-called moral problems—such as gay marriage—where no real suffering is at issue, and they will happily contribute to the surplus of human misery if it serves their religious beliefs.

Dogma Impedes Wisdom

A case in point: embryonic-stem-cell research is one of the most promising developments in the last century of medicine. It could offer therapeutic breakthroughs for every human ailment (for the simple reason that stem cells can become any tissue in the human body), including diabetes, Parkinson's disease, severe burns, etc. President George W. Bush used his first [presidential] veto to deny federal funding to this research. He did this on the basis of his religious faith. Like

FAST FACT

In 2006, Keith Ellison became the first Muslim to be elected to Congress.

millions of other Americans, President Bush believes that "human life starts at the moment of conception." Specifically, he believes that there is a soul in every 3-day-old human embryo, and the interests of one soul—the soul of a little girl with burns over 75 percent of her body, for instance—cannot trump the interests of another soul, even if that soul happens to live inside a petri dish. Here, as ever, religious dogmatism impedes genuine wisdom and compassion.

A 3-day-old human embryo is a collection of 150 cells called a blastocyst. There are, for the sake of comparison, more than 100,000 cells in the brain of a fly. The embryos that are destroyed in stem-cell research do not have brains, or even neurons. Consequently, there is no reason to believe they can suffer their destruction in any way at all. The truth is that President Bush's unjustified religious beliefs about the human soul are, at this very moment, prolonging the scarcely endurable misery of tens of millions of human beings.

God Approves Policy

Given our status as a superpower, our material wealth and the continuous advancements in our technology, it seems safe to say that the president of the United States has more power and responsibility than any person in history. It is worth noting, therefore, that we have elected a president who seems to imagine that whenever he closes his eyes in the Oval Office—wondering whether to go to war or not to go to war, for instance—his intuitions have been vetted by the Creator of the universe. Speaking to a small group of supporters in 1999, Bush reportedly said, "I believe God wants me to be president." Believing that God has delivered you unto the presidency really seems to entail the belief that you cannot make any catastrophic mistakes while in office. One question we might want to collectively ponder in the future: do we really want to hand the tiller of civilization to a person who thinks this way?

Dangerous Beliefs

Religion is the one area of our discourse in which people are systematically protected from the demand to give good evidence and valid arguments in defense of their strongly held beliefs. And yet these beliefs regularly determine what they live for, what they will die for and—all too often—what they will kill for. Consequently, we are living in a world in which millions of grown men and women can rationalize the violent sacrifice of their own children by recourse to fairy tales. We are living in a world in which millions of Muslims believe that there is nothing better than to be killed in defense of Islam. We are living in a world in which millions of Christians hope to soon be raptured into the stratosphere by Jesus so that they can safely enjoy a sacred genocide that will inaugurate the end of human history. In a world brimming with increasingly destructive technology, our infatuation with religious myths now poses a tremendous danger. And it is not a danger for which more religious faith is a remedy.

EVALUATING THE AUTHOR'S ARGUMENTS:

After reading this viewpoint, do you agree that evidence and facts should be more important than religious beliefs in political decisions? Why or why not?

Facts About the U.S. Government

Budget

According to CNN:

- The amount spent annually by the U.S. government increased ten-fold from 1910 to 1920.
- The amount spent annually by the U.S. government fell by nearly one half from 1920 to 1930.
- The amount spent annually by the U.S. government nearly tripled from 1930 to 1940.
- The amount spent annually by the U.S. government increased by nearly five times from 1940 to 1950.
- The U.S. government's budget more than doubled between 1960 and 1970.
- The U.S. government's budget more than tripled between 1970 and 1980.
- The U.S. government's budget more than doubled between 1980 and 1990.
- The U.S. government's budget in 2002 was more than 2,708 times as much as the budget in 1910.
- As reported in newspapers, on September 10, 2001, defense secretary Donald Rumsfeld announced that $2.3 trillion dollars in money allocated to the Pentagon could not be accounted for: roughly $8,000 for every man, woman, and child in America.

Presidential Veto

When the president is presented a bill adopted by both houses of Congress, he can either sign it into law, veto it, or fail to sign it within ten days, which has the effect of a veto and is called a "pocket veto." A veto can be overridden by a two-thirds majority vote by Congress.

- The first president, George Washington, vetoed 2 bills.
- Only five presidents have vetoed more than 100 bills: Franklin Delano Roosevelt vetoed 635 bills; Grover Cleveland vetoed 414 bills; Harry Truman vetoed 250 bills; Dwight Eisenhower vetoed 181 bills; and Grover Cleveland (in his other term) vetoed 170 bills.

- Only seven presidents never vetoed a bill: John Adams, Thomas Jefferson, John Quincy Adams, William Harrison, Zachary Taylor, Millard Fillmore, and James Garfield.
- President George W. Bush has vetoed fewer bills than any president since Warren Harding (who served from 1921 to 1923) and is the first since Harding to veto fewer than 10 bills.
- Only three presidents have had ten or more vetoes overridden: Andrew Johnson had fifteen vetoes overridden and Harry Truman and Gerald Ford each had twelve vetoes overridden.
- The following presidents who vetoed at least 1 bill never had their vetoes overridden: James Madison, John Monroe, James Polk, James Buchanan, William McKinley, Warren Harding, John F. Kennedy, Lyndon Johnson, and George W. Bush.
- Of a total of 2,553 presidential vetoes, only 106 have been overridden by Congress.

Impeachment

The process for impeachment of federal officials appears in Article I, Section 3, of the Constitution. Impeachment is a legal statement by the House of Representatives of charges that, if true, can be grounds for removing an official from office. After impeachment occurs, there is a trial in the Senate, with a two-thirds majority vote required to convict. Since adoption of the U.S. Constitution:

- Impeachment proceedings have been initiated over sixty times in the House of Representatives.
- There have been sixteen impeachments of federal officials.
- Twelve of the sixteen impeachments were of federal judges.
- One cabinet member has been impeached, secretary of war William Belknap in 1876.
- The first impeachment occurred in 1799, of William Blount, a Tennessee senator.
- Only two presidents have been impeached, Andrew Johnson in 1868 and William Clinton in 1999. Neither were convicted.
- There have been eight convictions, all of them judges.

Constitutional Amendments
- Of more than ten thousand amendments to the U.S. Constitution that have been proposed, only 27 have been adopted.

- Eleven of the amendments to the U.S. Constitution were adopted prior to 1800.
- Four of the amendments were adopted during the nineteenth century.
- No amendments have been adopted during the twenty-first century; the last amendment, adopted in 1992, concerning congressional pay raises was originally proposed in the eighteenth century.

Women in U.S. Government

According to the Center for American Women in Politics:

- Susanna Salter was the first woman mayor in the United States, elected in Argonia, Kansas, in 1887.
- Two women, Victoria Woodhull and Belva Lockwood, ran for president in the nineteenth century.
- Three women were elected to the Colorado House of Representatives in 1894, becoming the first women elected to any state legislature.
- Jeannette Rankin, a Republican from Montana, became the first woman elected to Congress in 1917.
- Nellie Ross, a Wyoming Democrat , was the first woman elected governor, in 1925.
- Shirley Chisholm became the first black woman to serve in Congress, in 1968.
- Sandra Day O'Connor, in 1981, was the first woman appointed to the U.S. Supreme Court.
- Janet Reno, in 1993, was the first woman appointed to serve as U.S. Attorney General.
- Madeleine Albright, in 1997, became the first woman to serve as U.S. secretary of state.
- Condoleezza Rice became the first woman to hold the post of National Security Advisor, in 2001.
- Nancy Pelosi was elected House Democratic Whip in 2001, the highest-ranking woman in the history of the U.S. Congress; in 2006 she became the first woman to become Speaker of the House.

Glossary

Bill of Rights: The first ten amendments to the Constitution. These amendments enumerate limitations on governmental power in order to protect the freedoms of citizens.

democracy: A system of government in which power is vested in the people, who exercise that power directly or indirectly through freely elected representatives.

executive: The branch of government charged with executing and enforcing the laws.

federalism: A system of government in which sovereignty is divided between a central or national government and constituent units, such as states or provinces.

freedom of religion: Freedom to believe and worship as one chooses, including freedom to not believe in any religion. The First Amendment to the U.S. Constitution prohibits Congress from making laws establishing religion or prohibiting the free exercise of religion.

impeachment: The first step in a process by which government officials can be removed from office for certain types of misconduct.

judicial: The branch of government charged with interpreting and applying the law to specific controversies between parties.

judicial review: The power of the judicial branch of government to review the constitutionality of actions taken or laws adopted by the other branches of government.

legislative: The branch of government having the power to make or enact laws, levy taxes, and make financial appropriations.

lobbyist: Individual who attempts to influence public officials to act in ways favorable to the special interests represented by the lobbyist.

oligarchy: A system of government in which a small group of people exercise governance.

religious test: A requirement that a public official, to be qualified to hold office, must have or not have certain religious or theological beliefs. The U.S. Constitution prohibits religious tests.

separation of church and state: The idea or doctrine that government and religious institutions should be kept separate and independent of each other.

separation of powers: A feature of a state in which government is divided into branches, each having separate and independent powers.

theocracy: Government of a state by divine guidance or by officials regarded as being divinely guided.

veto: The power of the executive branch to nullify laws enacted by the legislative branch.

Organizations to Contact

The editors have compiled the following list of organizations concerned with the issues debated in this book. The descriptions are derived from materials provided by the organizations. All have publications or information available for interested readers. The list was compiled on the date of publication of the present volume; the information provided here may change. Be aware that many organizations take several weeks or longer to respond to inquiries, so allow as much time as possible.

Acton Institute for the Study of Religion & Liberty

161 Ottawa Ave. NW, Ste. 301, Grand Rapids, MI 49503
(616) 454-3080 • fax: (616) 454-9454
e-mail: info@acton.org
Web site: www.acton.org
The Acton Institute is named after the English historian, John Lord Acton (1834–1902) best known for his remark that "power tends to corrupt, and absolute power corrupts absolutely." The mission of the Acton Institute is to promote a free and virtuous society characterized by individual liberty and sustained by religious principles. The institute conducts seminars and publishes books, monographs, periodicals, and articles, including ones pertaining to religion and U.S. government.

American Civil Liberties Union (ACLU)

125 Broad St., 18th Fl.
New York, NY 10004
(212) 549-2585
Web site: www.aclu.org
The American Civil Liberties Union promotes the protection of individual liberties guaranteed by the US. Constitution against unlawful exercise of government power. The ACLU's Web site has articles and information on issues concerning unconstitutional exercise of power by the executive and legislative branches of government as well as

information on court cases that interpret the Constitution. The ACLU also provides information on how citizens can make known their views on legislation that affects individual freedoms.

Americans United for Separation of Church and State (AU)
518 C St. NE, Washington, DC 20002
(202) 466-3234 • fax (202) 466-2587
e-mail: americansunited@au.org
Web site: www.au.org
The AU works to protect separation of church and state by working on a wide range of pressing political and social issues, including religion in the schools, religious symbols on public property, church electioneering, and religion in public life. Research and resource materials on these issues can be found on the group's Web site.

Brookings Institution
1775 Massachusetts Ave. NW, Washington, DC 20036-2188
e-mail: brookinfo@brook.edu
Web site: www.brook.edu
The Brookings Institution is a private, nonprofit organization that conducts research on economics, education, foreign and domestic government policy, and the social sciences. It publishes the quarterly *Brookings Review* and many books through its publishing division, the Brookings Institution Press. Articles pertaining to U.S. government can be accessed on its Web site.

Cato Institute
1000 Massachusetts Ave. NW, Washington, DC 20001-5403
e-mail: cato@cato.org
Web site: www.cato.org
The Cato Institute is a libertarian public policy research foundation dedicated to limiting the role of government and protecting individual liberties. The Cato Institute is named after Cato's Letters, a series of libertarian pamphlets that the institute's founders say helped lay the philosophical foundation for the American Revolution. The institute's searchable database allows access to a number of articles on U.S. government.

Common Cause
1133 Nineteenth St. NW, 9th Fl.
Washington, DC 20036
(202) 833-1200
Web site: www.commoncause.org
Common Cause promotes honest, open, and accountable government and citizen participation in the functioning of U.S. government. The issues the group focuses on include voting, increased citizen participation, media consolidation, and campaign reform. The group's Web site has articles on these topics and information on how to register to vote.

The Heritage Foundation
214 Massachusetts Ave. NE
Washington DC 20002-4999
(202) 546-4400 • fax: (202) 546-8328
e-mail: info@heritage.org
Web site: www.heritage.org
The Heritage Foundation is a conservative think tank that promotes public policy based on limited government and individual freedom. The organization's Web site has a searchable database that includes many articles about U.S. government.

Institute on Religion and Democracy (IRD)
1023 Fifteenth St. NW, Ste. 601
Washington, DC 2005-2601
(202) 682-4131 • fax: (202) 682-4136
Web site: www.ird-renew.org
The Institute on Religion and Democracy is an ecumenical religious group promoting social activism consistent with biblical and historical Christian teachings. IRD's Web site has a variety of articles on the environment, life issues, marriage and family, the Middle East, and world peace.

Judicial Watch

PO Box 44444

Washington, DC 20026

(888) 593-8442 • fax: (202) 646-5199Web site: www.judicialwatch.org

Judicial Watch is a conservative nonpartisan organization dedicated to preventing abuse of power by political and judicial officials and to promoting transparency, accountability, and fidelity to the rule of law. The group performs its mission through education, public outreach, investigations, and litigation. The group's Web site has publications and news links on issues concerning potential illegal exercise of government power. Judicial Watch has filed more than 150 lawsuits against federal, state, and local officials and agencies throughout the nation.

The Pew Forum on Religion & Public Life

1615 L St. NW, Ste. 700, Washington DC 20036

(202) 419-4550 • fax: (202) 419-4559

Web site: www.pewforum.org

The forum seeks to promote a deeper understanding of issues at the intersection of religion and public affairs. It provides information on this subject to national opinion leaders, including government officials and journalists. As a nonpartisan, nonadvocacy organization, the forum does not take positions on policy debates. Its Web site includes many articles on the relationship between religion and government.

For Further Reading

Books

Dennis Brindell, *The Declaration of Independence*. New York: Marshall Cavendish/Benchmark, 2007. Discusses how the Declaration of Independence came to be written and the effect it had on creation of U.S. government.

Harold H. Bruff, *Balance of Forces: Separation of Powers Law in the Administrative State*. Durham, NC: Carolina Academic Press, 2006. Argues that balance of power in government is an evolving situation and summarizes lessons drawn from constitutional history and different approaches to analyzing accountability and the limits of executive and judicial power.

Catherine Crier, *Contempt: How the Right Is Wronging American Justice*. New York: Rugged Land, 2005. Argues that the Christian Right poses a threat to the federal judiciary and the separation of powers that is fundamental to U.S. government.

Newt Gingrich, *Rediscovering God in America*. Nashville: Integrity House, 2006. Describes author's view of the role God and religion have played historically in the creation and functioning of U.S. government.

John C. Green, *The Faith Factor: How Religion Influences American Elections*. Westport, CT: Praeger, 2007. Documents the changing role of religion in American politics over the last sixty years and probes the meaning of religious belonging, behaving, and believing as well as how these three areas affect election outcomes.

Al Gore, *The Assault on Reason*. New York: Penguin, 2007. Argues that due to various factors, reasoned discourse no longer takes place in democracy and the danger this poses to the future of U.S. government.

Katy J. Harriger, *Separation of Powers: Documents and Commentary*. Washington, DC: CQ Press, 2003. Describes the origins, purpose, and importance of the concept of separation of powers in U.S. government, quoting from the writings of political philosophers, America's founding documents, congressional debates, presidential statements, and Supreme Court decisions.

Barack Obama, *The Audacity of Hope: Thoughts on Reclaiming the American Dream*. New York: Crown, 2006. Describes the author's thoughts on America, politics, and what he believes is Americans' hope for the future of the U.S. government.

Kermit Roosevelt III, *The Myth of Judicial Activism: Making Sense of Supreme Court Decisions*. New Haven, CT: Yale University Press, 2007. Argues that the Supreme Court usually does not abuse its power but instead properly defers to the judgment of other branches of government.

Periodicals

Peter Baker, "Bush Retreats on Use of Executive Power: Allowing Court's Role Is Latest Step Back," *Washington Post*, January 18, 2007.

Sandra Beasley, "Higher Powers That Be: The Relationship Between Religion and the Government in the USA," *American Scholar*, January 1, 2007.

Jeffrey H. Birnbaum, "Don't Cry for Republican Lobbyists, *Washington Post*, November 13, 2006.

Clint Bolick, "A Cheer for Judicial Activism," *Wall Street Journal*, April 3, 2007.

Karen Brooks, "Selling Lobbyists on Ethics: Austin Seminar Reminds Hundreds How to Behave with Lawmakers," *Dallas Morning News*, September 16, 2006.

Randall K. Bush, "Religion, Politics, and the Christian Right: Post 9/11 Powers and American Empire; The Left Hand of God; Taking Back Our Country from the Religious Right," *Theology Today*, July 2007.

M. A. Casey, "Democracy and the Thin Veneer of Civilization, *Quadrant*, November 1, 2006.

Dimitri Cavalli, "A Liberal Mix of Religion and Politics," *Wall Street Journal*, June 8, 2007.

Christian Century, "Half of U.S. Evangelicals Do Not Support Government Funding of Faith-Based Organizations, a Survey Shows," November 28, 2006.

Tim Conlan and John Dinan, "Federalism, the Bush Administration, and the Transformation of Conservatism," *Publius*, Summer 2007.

Maeve Cooke, "A Secular State for a Post-Secular Society? Post-Metaphysical Political Theory and the Place of Religion," *Constellations: An International Journal of Critical and Democratic Theory*," June 2007.

Joseph Deering, "Politics as a Christian Vocation: Faith and Democracy Today, *Critical Sociology*, vol. 33, no. 3, 2007.

Nancy Gibbs, "The Religion Test," *Time*, May 21, 2007.

Dan Gligoff, "The Preacher Who Put God in Politics," *U.S. News & World Report*, May 28, 2007.

John Harrington, "Learning to Love the Lobbyists," *Helena (MT) Independent Record*, February 18, 2007.

Daniel Kelly, "Let's Not Tolerate Judicial Activism," *Madison (WI) Capitol Times*, March 1, 2007.

Dale Krane, "The Middle Tier in American Federalism: State Government Policy Activism During the Bush Presidency," *Publius*, Summer 2007.

Neil Kumar, "Internal Separation of Powers: Checking Today's Most Dangerous Branch from Within," *Yale Law Journal*, July 1, 2006.

Simon Lazarus, "More Polarizing than Rehnquist. Chief Justice John Roberts Won Senate Confirmation by Vowing to Shun Ideological Activism. Instead, by Trashing Judicial Precedent and Legislative Statutes, He's Reshaping Law to Fit Conservative Dogma," *American Prospect*, May 1, 2007.

Jonathan Macey, "Executive Branch Usurpation of Power: Corporations and Capital Markets," *Yale Law Journal*, July 1, 2006.

Pauline Maier, "Why Faith Plagues Us So: From the Beginning the U.S. Has Sought Ways to Balance Religion and Public Policy, and the Results Have Been Good and Bad," *Chicago Sun-Times*, May 21, 2006.

Jenny S. Martinez, "Inherent Executive Power: A Comparative Perspective," *Yale Law Journal*, July 1, 2006.

Thomas R. McFaul, "Religion in the Future Global Civilization: Globalization Is Intensifying Religious Conflicts. What Will Happen in the Years Ahead?" *Futurist*, September 1, 2006.

Bill O'Reilly, "How Prevalent Is Judicial Activism?" *The O'Reilly Factor* (Fox News Network), January 2, 2007. www.foxnews.com/oreilly.

James Pinkerton, "The Left Will Pay for Judicial Activism," *Cincinnati Post*, November 3, 2006.

Betsy Wright Rhodes, "Oil and Water, Religion and Government Don't Mix," *Norfolk Virginian-Pilot*, July 15, 2006.

Aurelio Rojas, "You Want to Be a Lobbyist? Popular Course Lays Out Culture of Capitol," *Sacramento (CA) Bee*, January 27, 2007.

Dinah Stephen, "Executive Power Hot Topic at New Hampshire Forums," *Washington Times*, April 4, 2007.

Catherine McNicol Stock, "Righteous Indignation: Religion and the Populist Revolution," *American Historial Review*, June 2007.

Cass R. Sunstein, "Beyond *Marbury:* The Executive's Power to Say What the Law Is," *Yale Law Journal*, July 1, 2006.

U.S. Newswire, "Exploring the Limits of Presidential Power After 9/11: Lessons from Abraham Lincoln's Use of Executive Power During the Civil War," January 3, 2006.

George F. Will, "About Those Categories: In the Roberts Court's First Major Decision, the Ideas of Liberalism, Conservatism, Activism and Deference to Democracy Got Blurred," *Newsweek*, January 30, 2006.

Frank J. Williams, "Civil Liberties v. National Security," *Civil War Times*, June 2007.

Joe Wolverton, "Presidential Power Grab: President Bush Has Been Quietly Attaching Pronouncements to Bills He Signs into Law. These Signing Statements Amount to a Grab for Legislative Power Belonging to Congress," *New American*, August 21, 2006.

Web Sites:

USA.gov (http://www.usa.gov). This is the U.S. government's official Web portal. It has information about government laws on virtually all areas, with links to federal, state, and local government agencies.

Center for American Women and Politics (http://www.cawp.rutgers .edu). This site has a great deal of information on women in U.S. government.

Common Dreams (http://www.commondreams.org). This Web site has news and information on politics and U.S. government from a progressive point of view.

Federalist Society (http://www.fed-soc.org). This site has resources and information that promote judicial restraint and libertarian and conservative views regarding the exercise of governmental power.

Fedstats (http://www.fedstats.gov). This site has a variety of downloadable statistics on federal and state governments and agencies.

Index

Picture Credits